THE GREAT HARMONICA SONGBOOK

45 SONGS SPECIALLY ARRANGED FOR DIATONIC HARMONICA

Arranged by Eric J. Plahna

ISBN 978-1-4234-5657-5

HAL•LEONARD®
CORPORATION

7777 W. BLUEMOUND RD. P.O. BOX 13819 MILWAUKEE, WI 53213

Visit Hal Leonard Online at
www.halleonard.com

HARMONICA NOTATION LEGEND

Harmonica music can be notated two different ways: on a *musical staff*, and in *tablature*.

THE MUSICAL STAFF shows pitches and rhythms and is divided by bar lines into measures. Pitches are named after the first seven letters of the alphabet.

TABLATURE graphically represents the harmonica music. Each note will be accompanied by a number, 1 through 10, indicating what hole you are to play. The arrow that follows indicates whether to blow or draw. (All examples are shown using a C diatonic harmonica.)

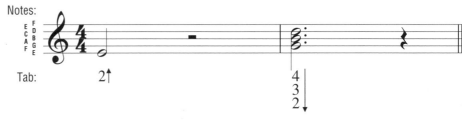

Blow (exhale) into 2nd hole.

Draw (inhale) 2nd, 3rd, & 4th holes together.

Notes on the C Harmonica

Exhaled (Blown) Notes

1	2	3	4	5	6	7	8	9	10
C	E	G	C	E	G	C	E	G	C

Inhaled (Drawn) Notes

1	2	3	4	5	6	7	8	9	10
D	G	B	D	F	A	B	D	F	A

Bends

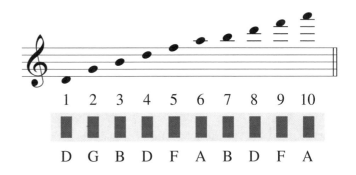

Blow Bends

- 1/4 step
- 1/2 step
- 1 step
- 1 1/2 steps

Draw Bends

- 1/4 step
- 1/2 step
- 1 step
- 1 1/2 steps

All My Loving

Words and Music by John Lennon and Paul McCartney

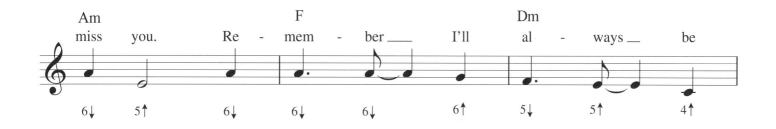

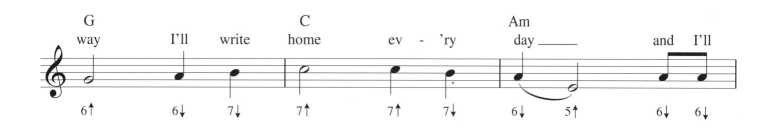

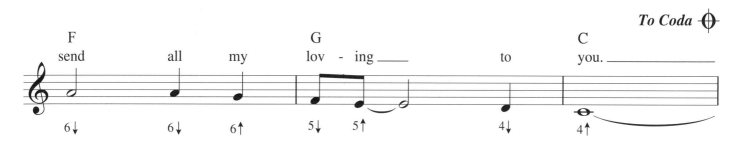

*Song sounds one octave higher than written.

Verse

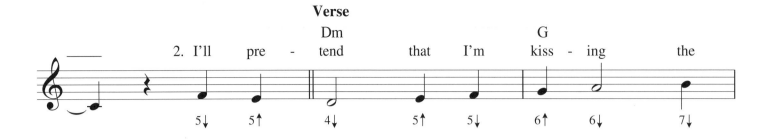

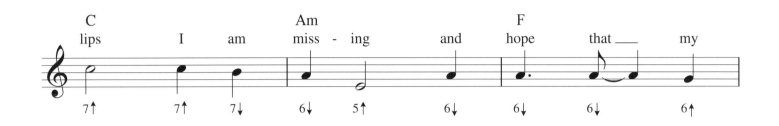

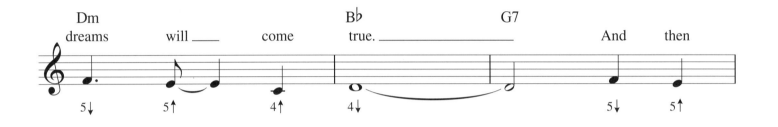

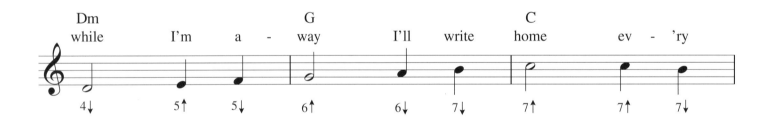

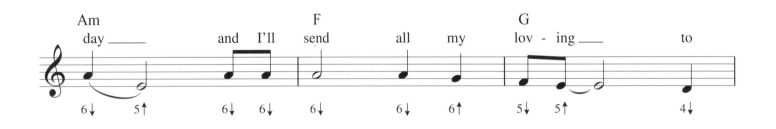

Chorus

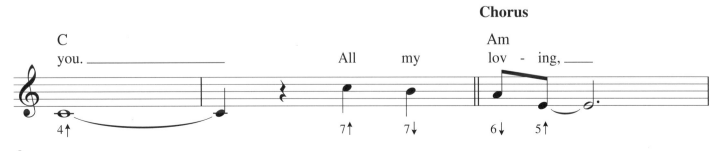

4

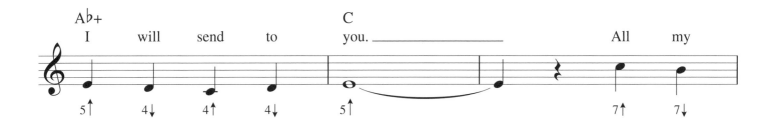

D.S. al Coda

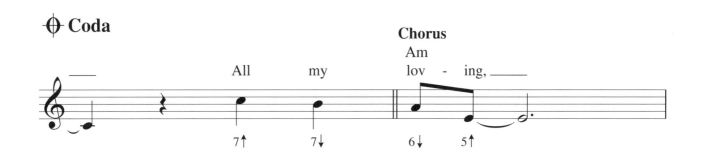

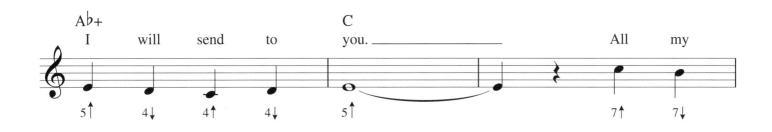

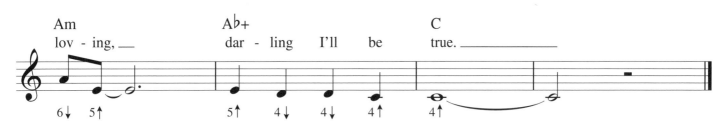

All I Ask of You

from THE PHANTOM OF THE OPERA
Music by Andrew Lloyd Webber
Lyrics by Charles Hart
Additional Lyrics by Richard Stilgoe

*Song sounds one octave higher than written.

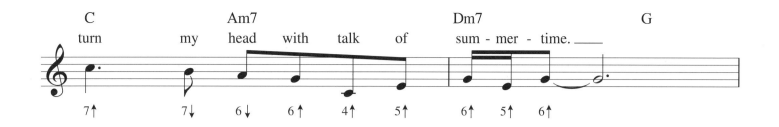

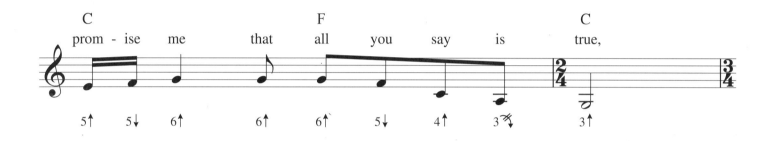

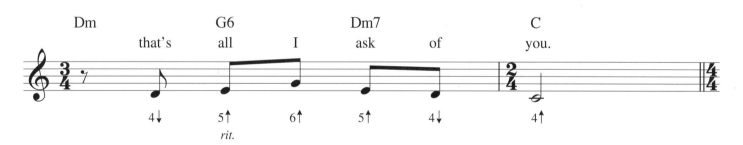

Verse
A tempo

Raoul:

C

Christine:

All I want is free-dom, a world with no more night; and

4↓ 4↑ 4↓ 5↑ 5↑ 3↑ 5↑ 4↓ 4↑ 4↓ 5↑ 6↑ 6↓

Cmaj7   F6   B♭   G

Raoul:

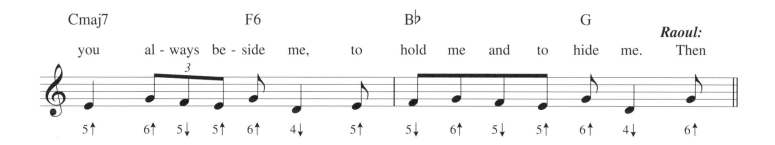

you al - ways be - side me, to hold me and to hide me. Then

5↑ 6↑ 5↓ 5↑ 6↑ 4↓ 5↑ 5↓ 6↑ 5↓ 5↑ 6↑ 4↓ 6↑

Chorus

C   Am7   Dm7   G

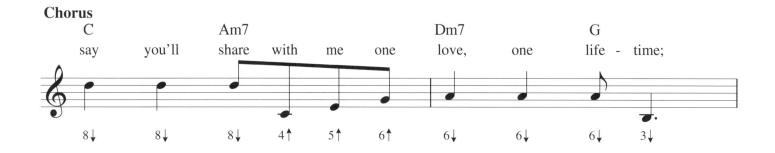

say you'll share with me one love, one life - time;

8↓ 8↓ 8↓ 4↑ 5↑ 6↑ 6↓ 6↓ 6↓ 3↓

C   Am7   Dm7   G7

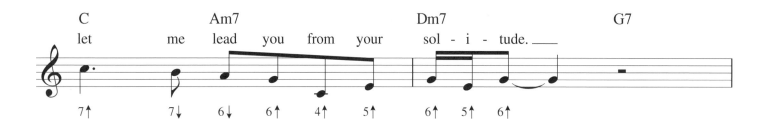

let me lead you from your sol - i - tude. ____

7↑ 7↓ 6↓ 6↑ 4↑ 5↑ 6↑ 5↑ 6↑

C   Am7   Dm7   G

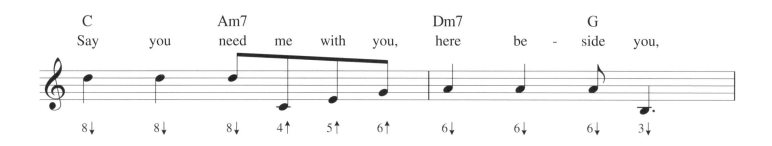

Say you need me with you, here be - side you,

8↓ 8↓ 8↓ 4↑ 5↑ 6↑ 6↓ 6↓ 6↓ 3↓

C   F   C

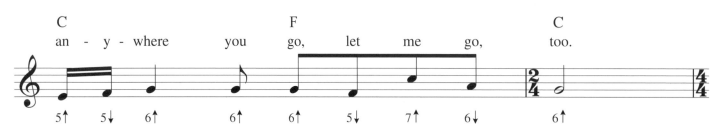

an - y - where you go, let me go, too.

5↑ 5↓ 6↑ 6↑ 6↑ 5↓ 7↑ 6↓ 6↑

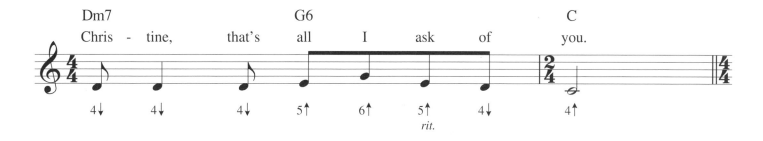

A tempo

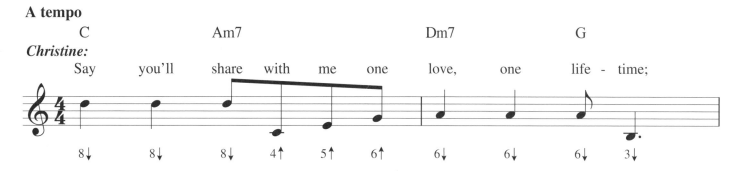

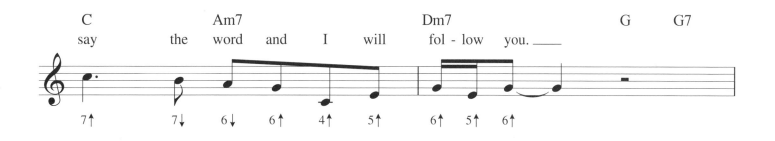

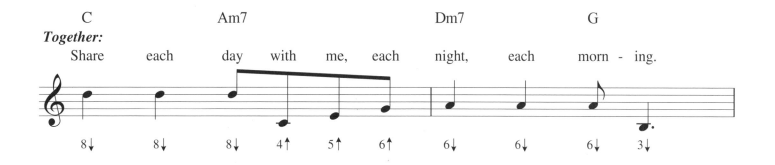

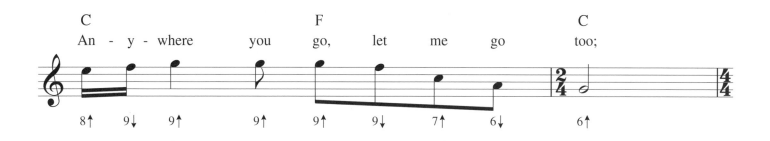

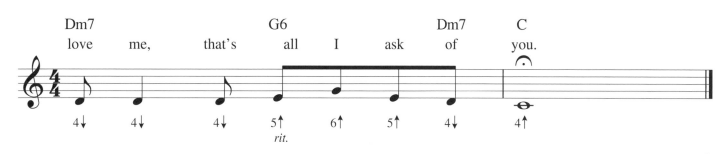

Beauty and the Beast

from Walt Disney's BEAUTY AND THE BEAST
Lyrics by Howard Ashman
Music by Alan Menken

Verse
Moderately slow

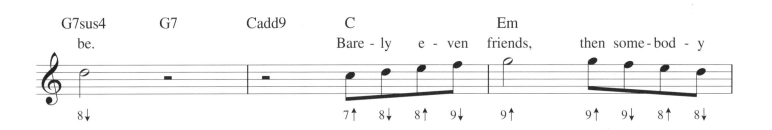

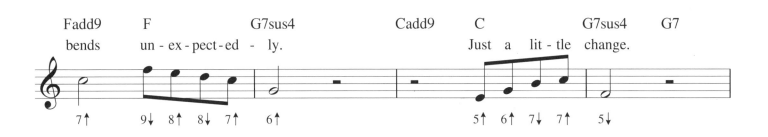

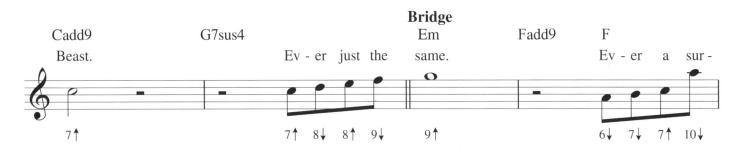

*Song sounds one octave higher than written.

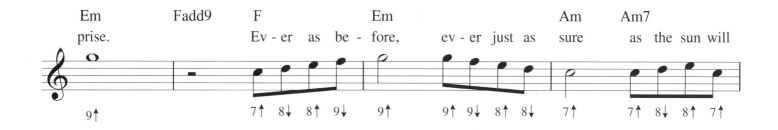

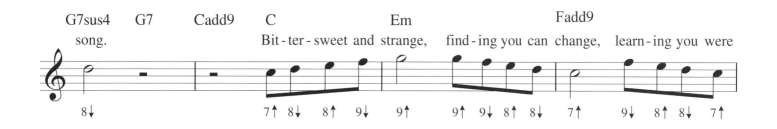
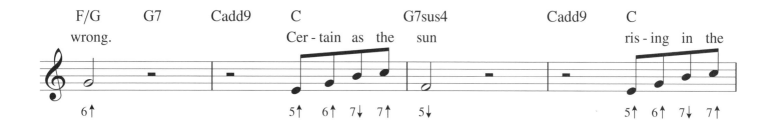
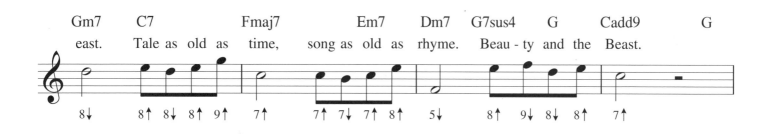
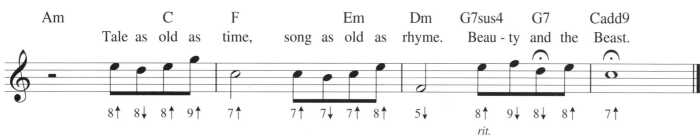

Brown Eyed Girl

Words and Music by Van Morrison

*Song sounds one octave higher than written.

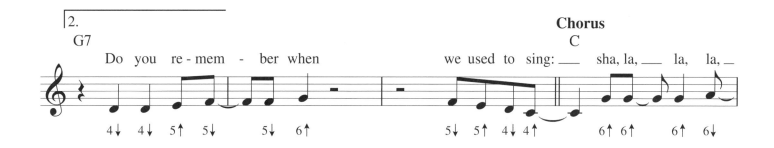

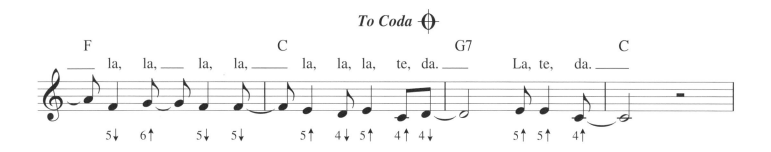

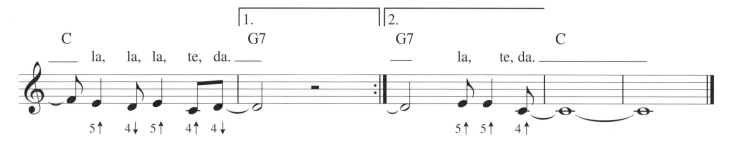

Additional Lyrics

2. Whatever happened to Tuesday and so slow?
   Going down the old mine with a transistor radio.
   Standing in the sunlight laughing,
   Hiding behind a rainbow's wall.
   Slipping and a sliding
   All along the waterfall
   With you, my brown eyed girl.
   You, my brown eyed girl.
   Do you remember when we used to sing:

3. So hard to find my way, now that I'm all on my own.
   I saw you just the other day, my, how you have grown.
   Cast my memory back there, Lord,
   Sometimes I'm overcome thinking 'bout it.
   Making love in the green grass
   Behind the stadium
   With you, my brown eyed girl.
   A you, my brown eyed girl.
   Do you remember when we used to sing:

Can You Feel the Love Tonight

from Walt Disney Pictures' THE LION KING
Music by Elton John
Lyrics by Tim Rice

Verse
Moderately slow

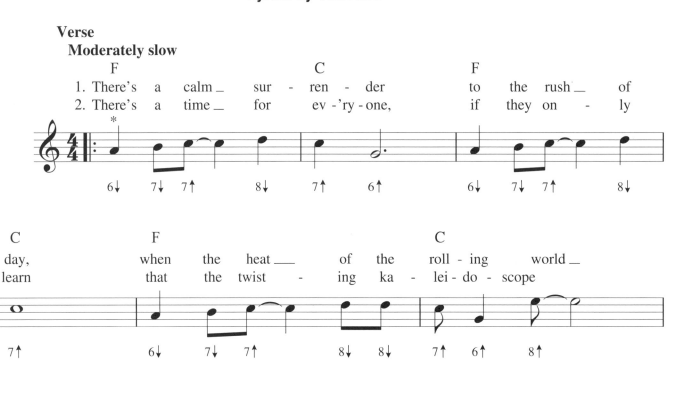

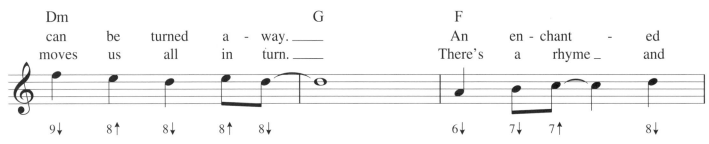

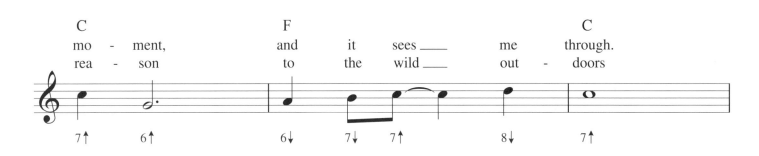

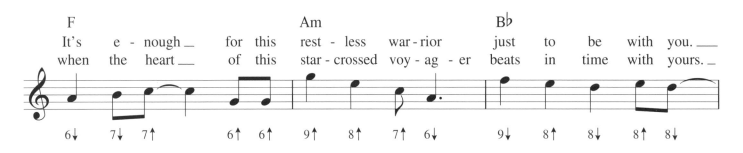

*Song sounds one octave higher than written.

Chorus

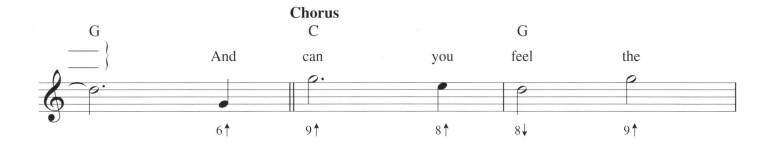

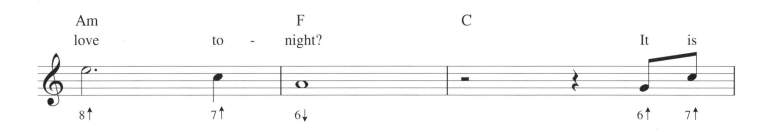

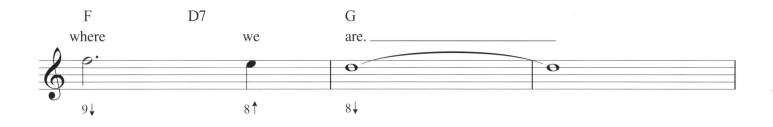

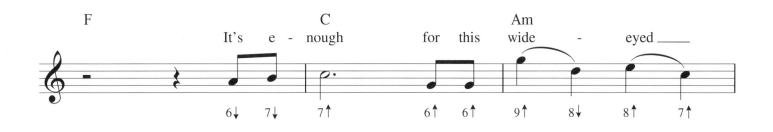

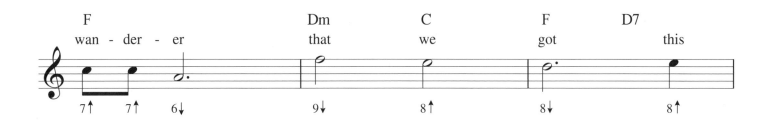

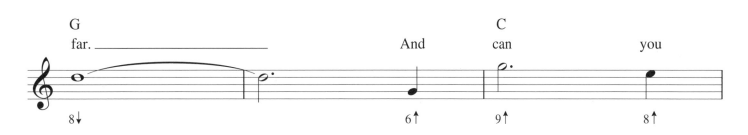

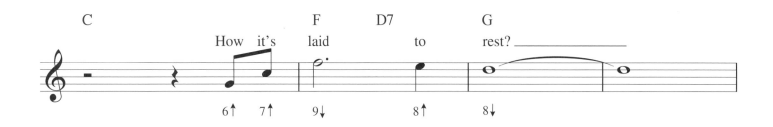

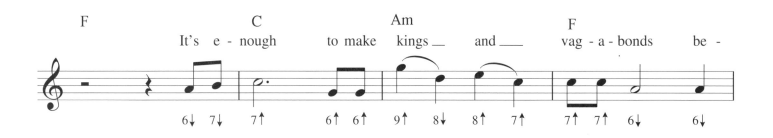

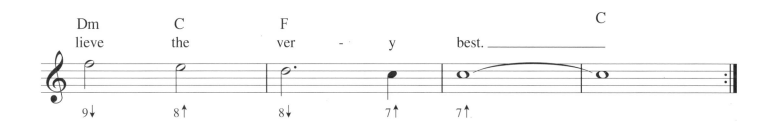

Outro

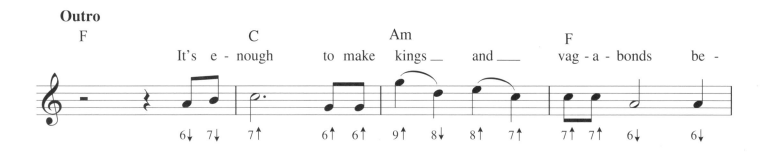

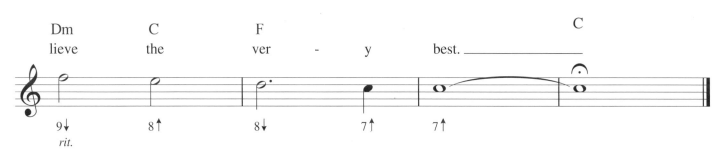

rit.

Edelweiss

from THE SOUND OF MUSIC
Lyrics by Oscar Hammerstein II
Music by Richard Rodgers

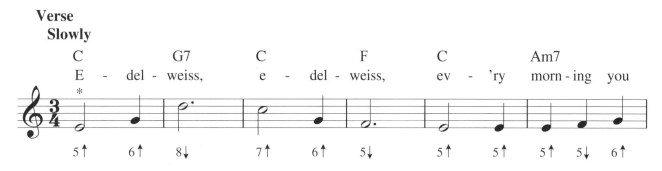

Verse
Slowly

E - del - weiss, e - del - weiss, ev - 'ry morn - ing you

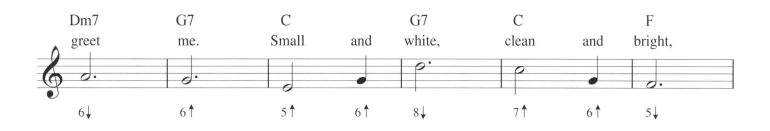

greet me. Small and white, clean and bright,

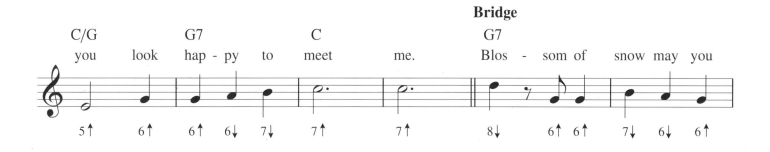

Bridge

you look hap - py to meet me. Blos - som of snow may you

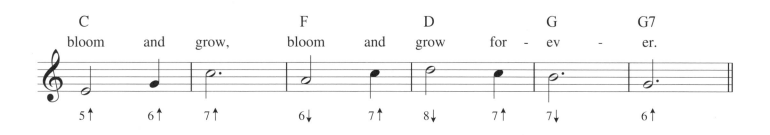

bloom and grow, bloom and grow for - ev - er.

Chorus

E - del - weiss, e - del - weiss, bless my home - land for - ev - er.

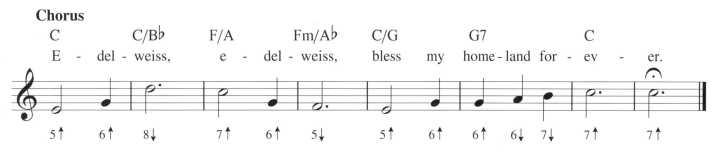

*Song sounds one octave higher than written.

Can't Help Falling in Love

from the Paramount Picture BLUE HAWAII
Words and Music by George David Weiss, Hugo Peretti and Luigi Creatore

*Song sounds one octave higher than written.

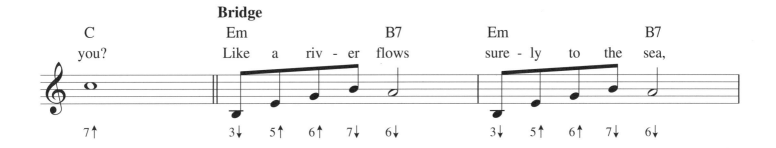

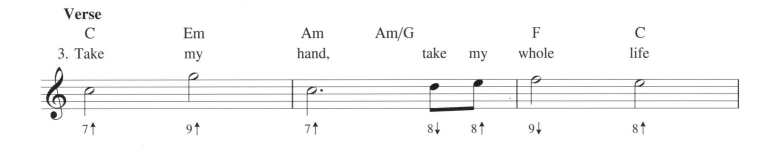

Verse

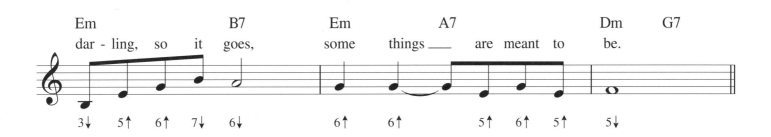

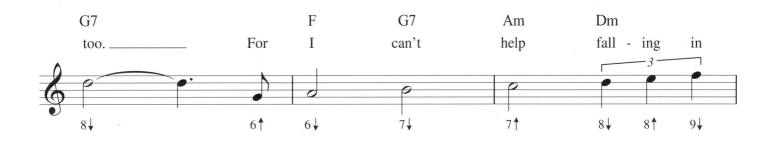

Outro

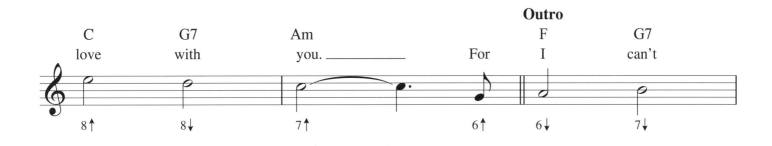

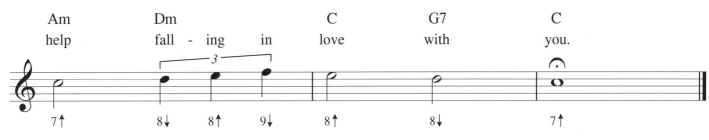

Daydream Believer

Words and Music by John Stewart

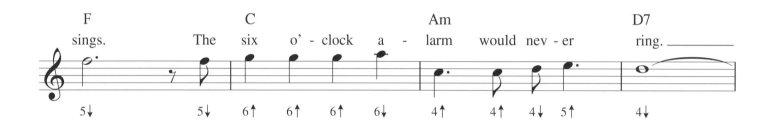

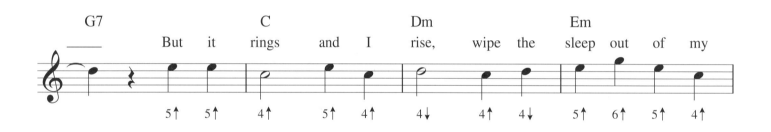

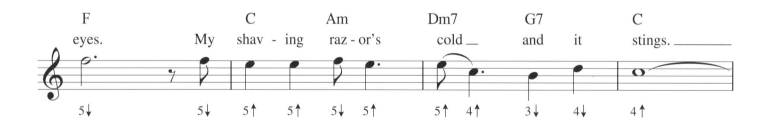

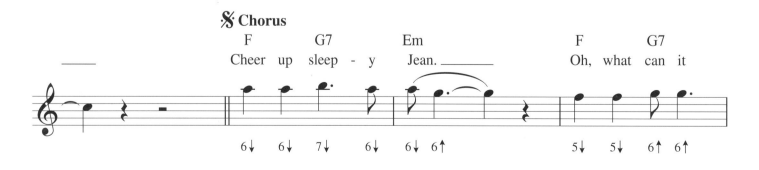

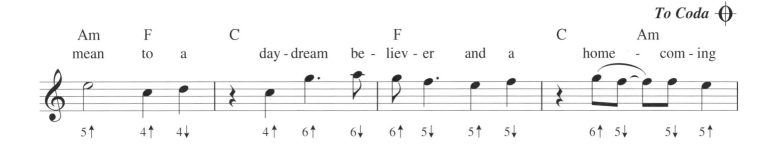

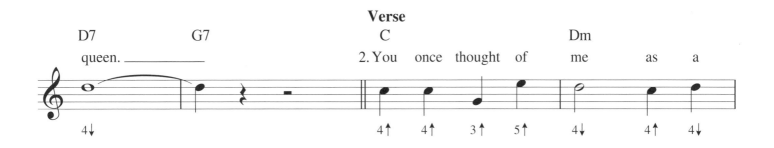

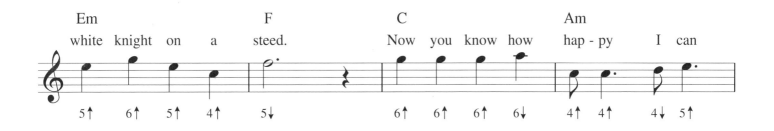

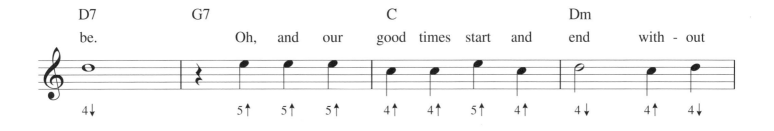

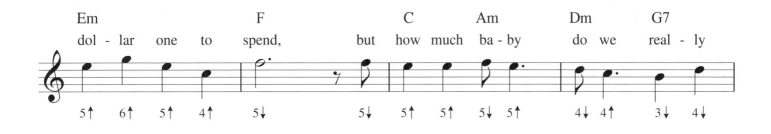

D.S. al Coda

⊕ **Coda**

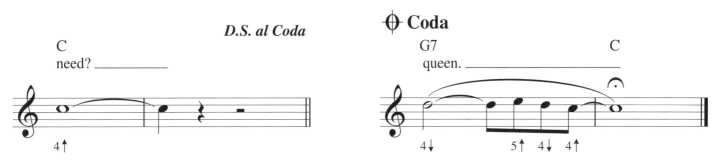

Don't Cry Out Loud

(We Don't Cry Out Loud)

Words and Music by Peter Allen and Carole Bayer Sager

*Song sounds one octave higher than written.

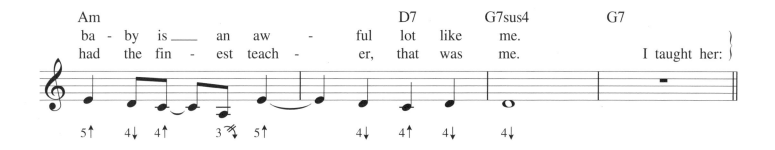

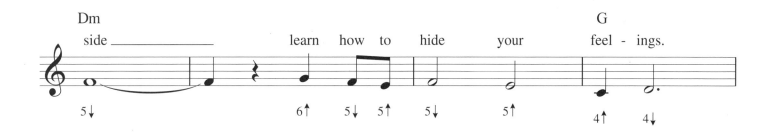

Chorus

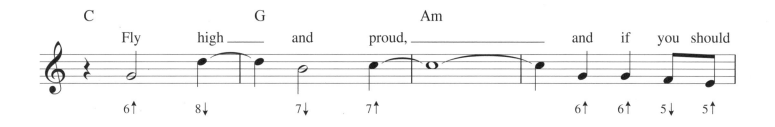

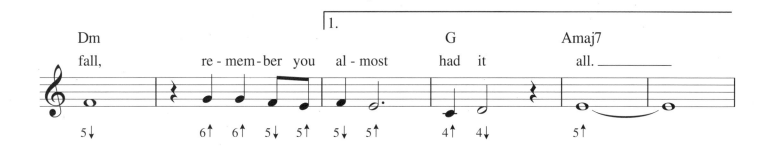

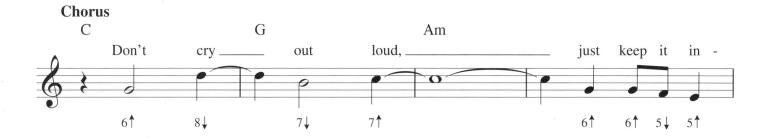

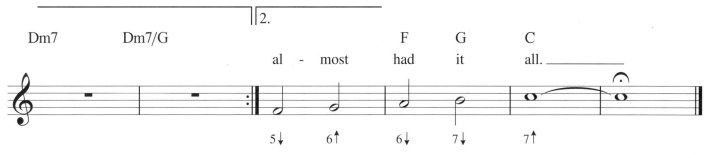

23

Duke of Earl

Words and Music by Earl Edwards, Eugene Dixon and Bernice Williams

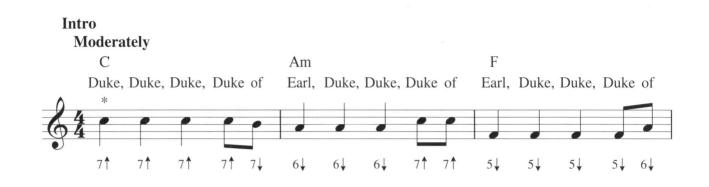

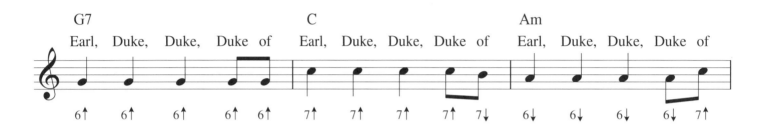

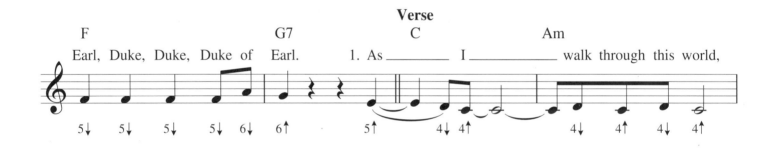

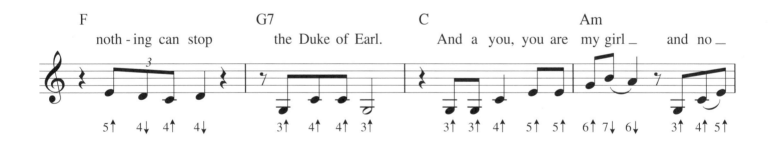

*Song sounds one octave higher than written.

Dust in the Wind

Words and Music by Kerry Livgren

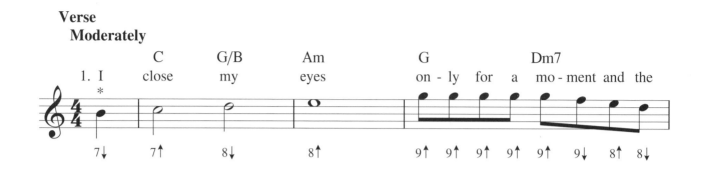

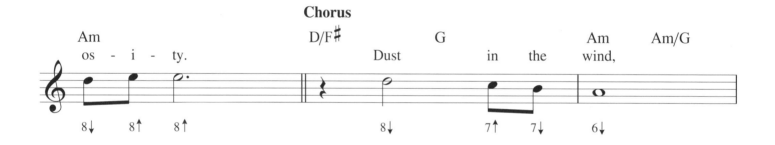

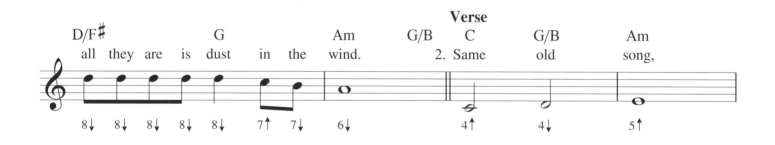

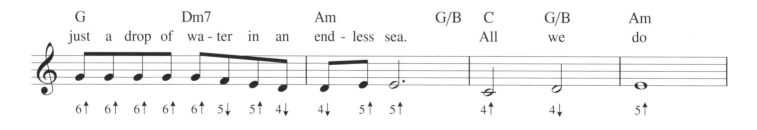

*Song sounds one octave higher than written.

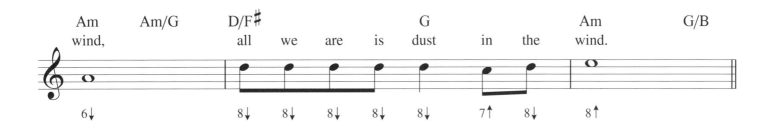

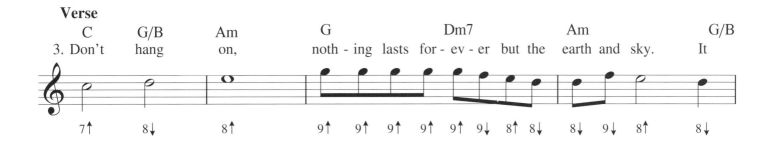

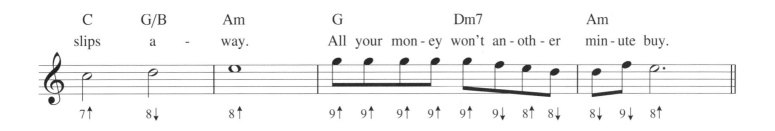

Chorus

Every Breath You Take

Music and Lyrics by Sting

Verse
Moderately

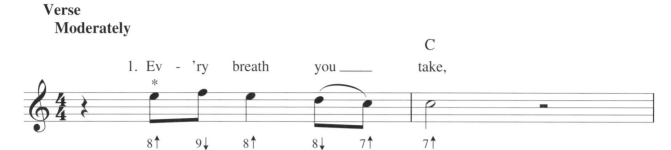

1. Ev - 'ry breath you take, (C)

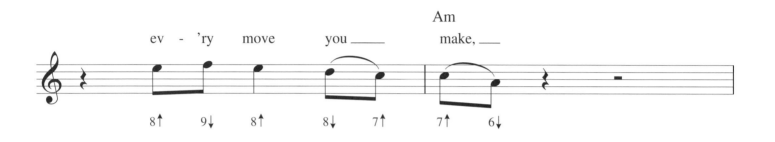

ev - 'ry move you make, (Am)

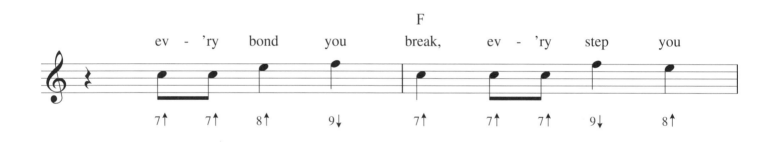

ev - 'ry bond you break, ev - 'ry step you (F)

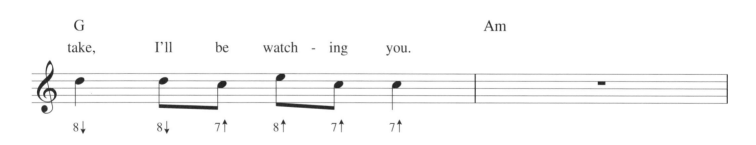

take, I'll be watch - ing you. (G ... Am)

Verse
C

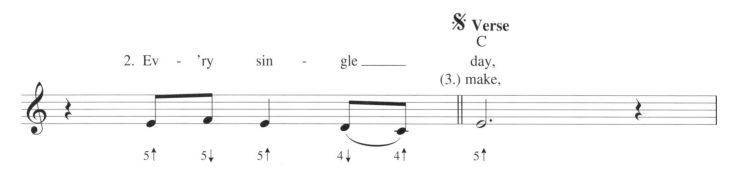

2. Ev - 'ry sin - gle day,
(3.) make,

*Song sounds one octave higher than written.

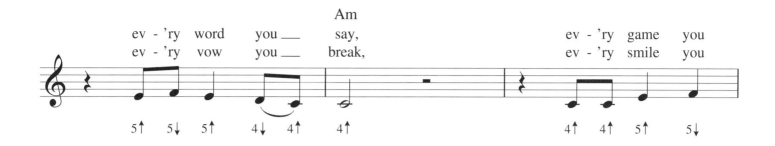

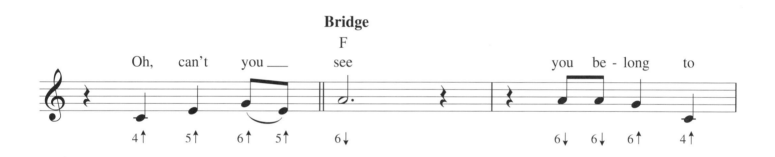

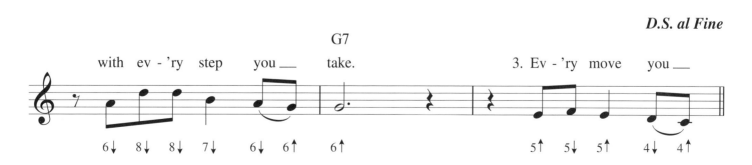

Heart and Soul

from the Paramount Short Subject A SONG IS BORN
Words by Frank Loesser
Music by Hoagy Carmichael

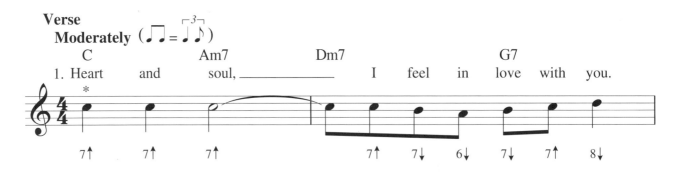

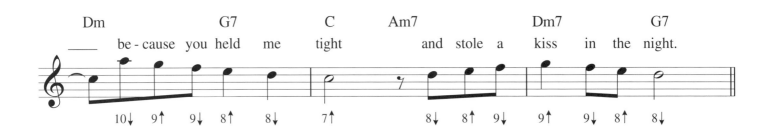

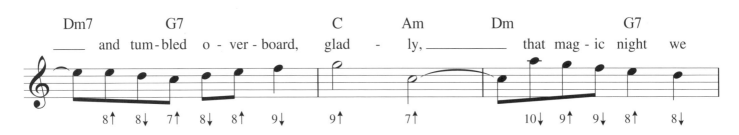

*Song sounds one octave higher than written.

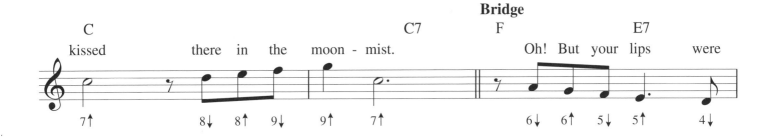

C   C7   F   E7

kissed   there in the moon - mist.   Oh! But your lips   were

7↑   8↓ 8↑ 9↓ 9↑   7↑   6↓ 6↑ 5↓ 5↑   4↓

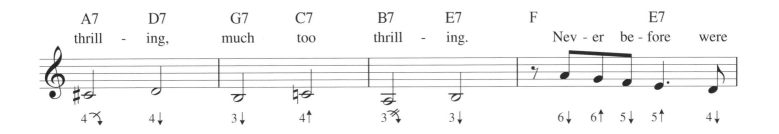

A7   D7   G7   C7   B7   E7   F   E7

thrill - ing,   much too   thrill - ing.   Nev - er be - fore   were

4↘   4↓   3↓   4↑   3↘   3↓   6↓ 6↑ 5↓ 5↑   4↓

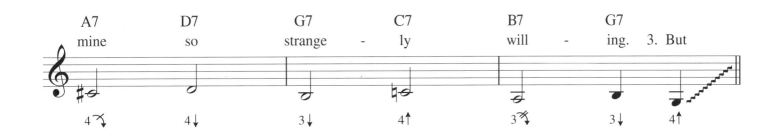

A7   D7   G7   C7   B7   G7

mine   so   strange - ly   will   -   ing. 3. But

4↘   4↓   3↓   4↑   3↘   3↓ 4↑

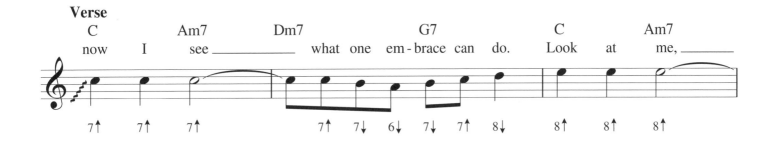

Verse

C   Am7   Dm7   G7   C   Am7

now I   see _____ what one em - brace can do.   Look at me, _____

7↑ 7↑ 7↑   7↑ 7↓ 6↓ 7↓ 7↑ 8↓   8↑   8↑   8↑

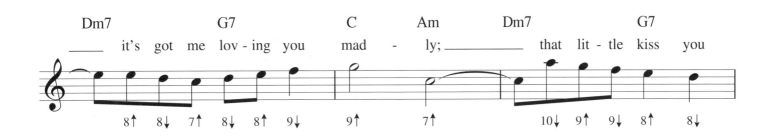

Dm7   G7   C   Am   Dm7   G7

____ it's got me lov - ing you mad - ly; _____ that lit - tle kiss you

8↑ 8↓ 7↑ 8↓ 8↑ 9↓   9↑   7↑   10↓ 9↑ 9↓ 8↑ 8↓

E7   A7   Dm   D9 G7   C

stole   held all my heart and   soul. _____

8↑   9↓ 8↑ 8↓ 7↑ 7↓   7↑

31

Help!

Words and Music by John Lennon and Paul McCartney

*Song sounds one octave higher than written.

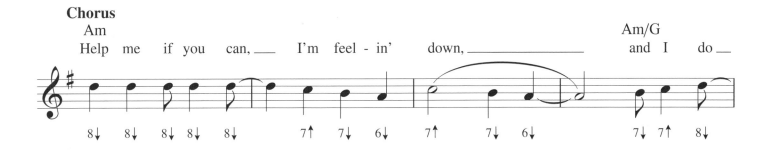

Chorus

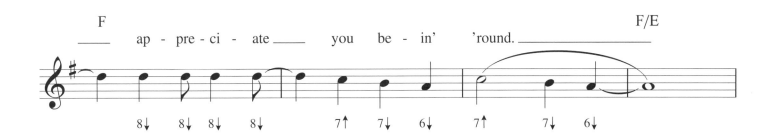

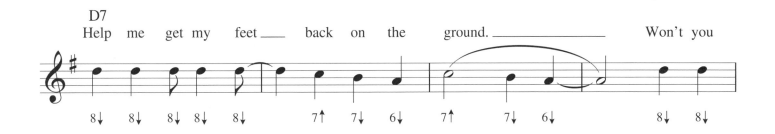

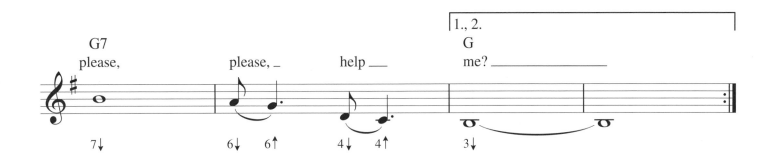

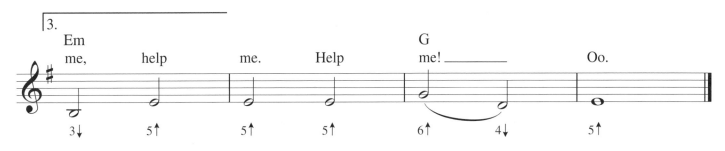

I Shot the Sheriff

Words and Music by Bob Marley

Intro
Moderate Reggae

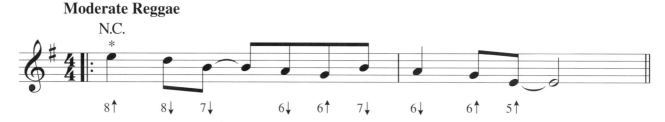

Chorus

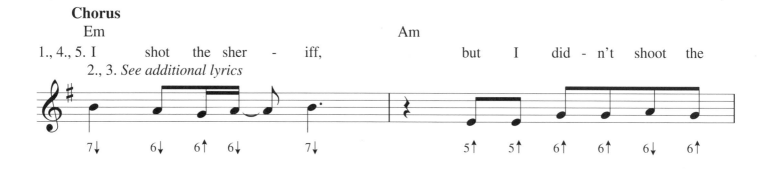

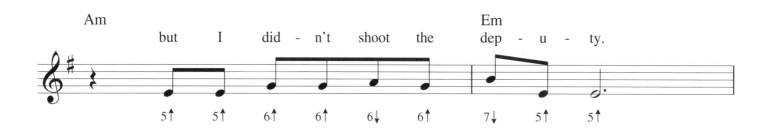

Fine **Verse**

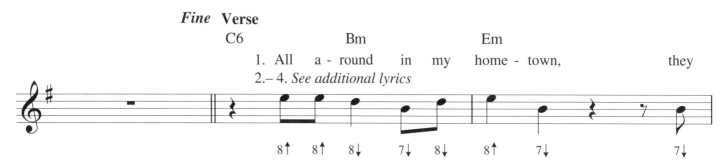

*Song sounds one octave higher than written.

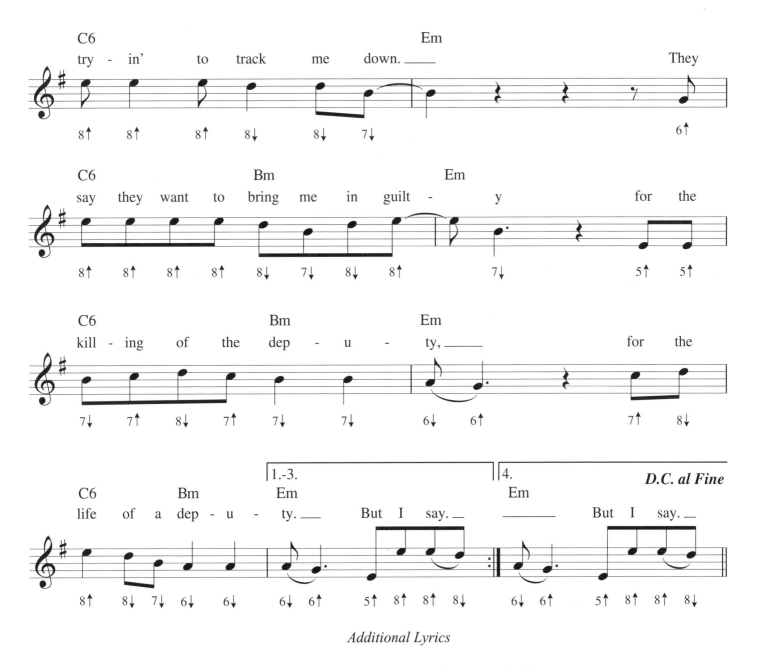

Additional Lyrics

Chorus 2. I shot the sheriff, but I swear it was in self defense.
I shot the sheriff, and they say it is a capital offense.

2. Sheriff John Brown always hated me.
For what, I don't know.
Ev'ry time I plant a seed,
He said, "Kill it before it grows."
He said, "Kill them before they grow."

Chorus 3. I shot the sheriff, but I swear it was in self defense.
I shot the sheriff, but I swear it was in self defense.

3. Freedom came my way, one day,
And I started out of town.
All of a sudden I saw Sheriff John Brown
Aimin' to shoot me down.
So I shot, I shot, I shot him down.

4. Reflexes had the better of me,
And what is to be, must be.
Ev'ry day the bucket a go a well,
One day the bottom of it drop out.
One day the bottom of it drop out.

I Walk the Line

Words and Music by John R. Cash

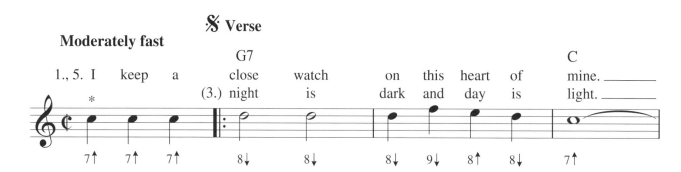

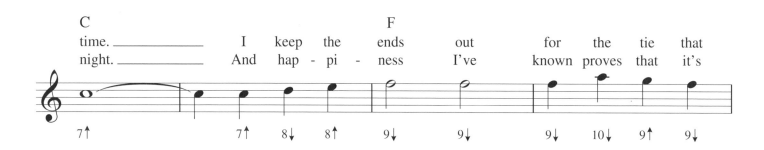

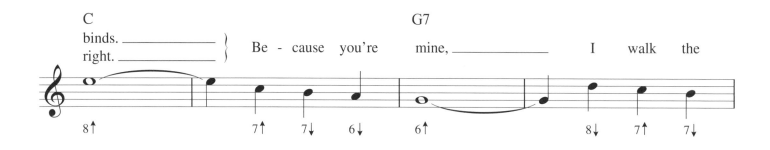

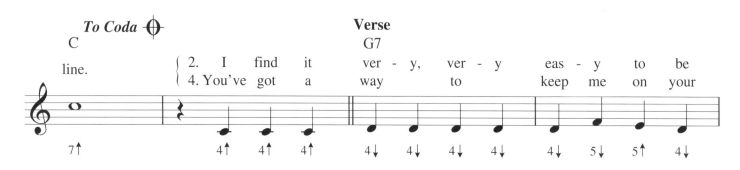

*Song sounds one octave higher than written.

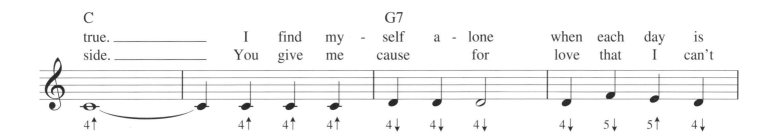

C   G7

true. _____ I find my - self a - lone when each day is
side. _____ You give me cause for love that I can't

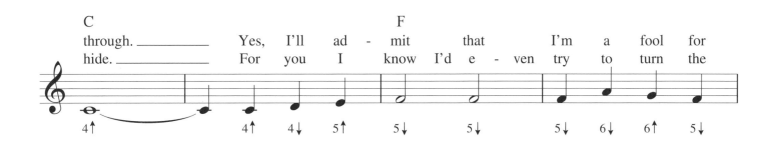

C   F

through. _____ Yes, I'll ad - mit that I'm a fool for
hide. _____ For you I know I'd e - ven try to turn the

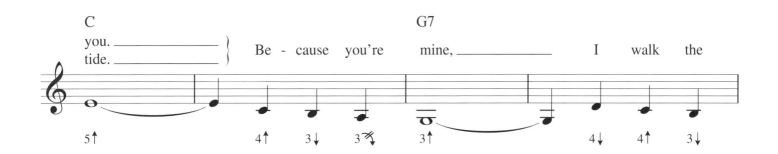

C   G7

you. _____ Be - cause you're mine, _____ I walk the
tide. _____

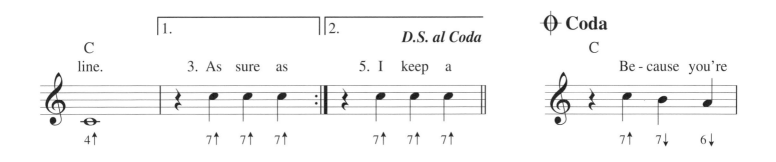

1.   2.   ***D.S. al Coda***   ⊕ **Coda**

C   C

line.   3. As sure as   5. I keep a   Be - cause you're

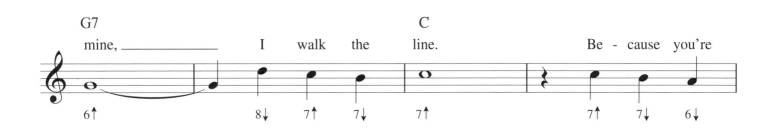

G7   C

mine, _____ I walk the line.   Be - cause you're

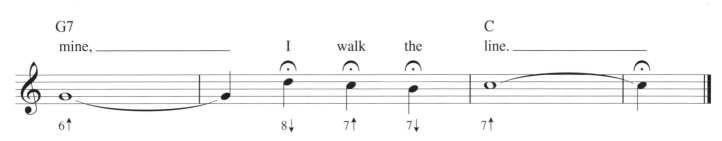

G7   C

mine, _____ I walk the line. _____

Imagine

Words and Music by John Lennon

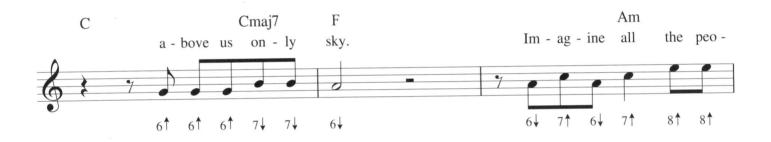

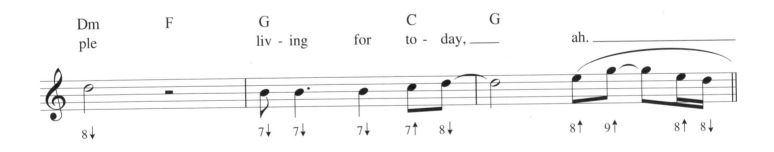

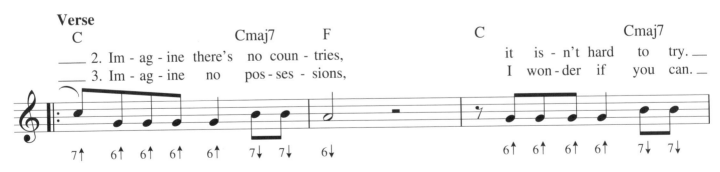

*Song sounds one octave higher than written.

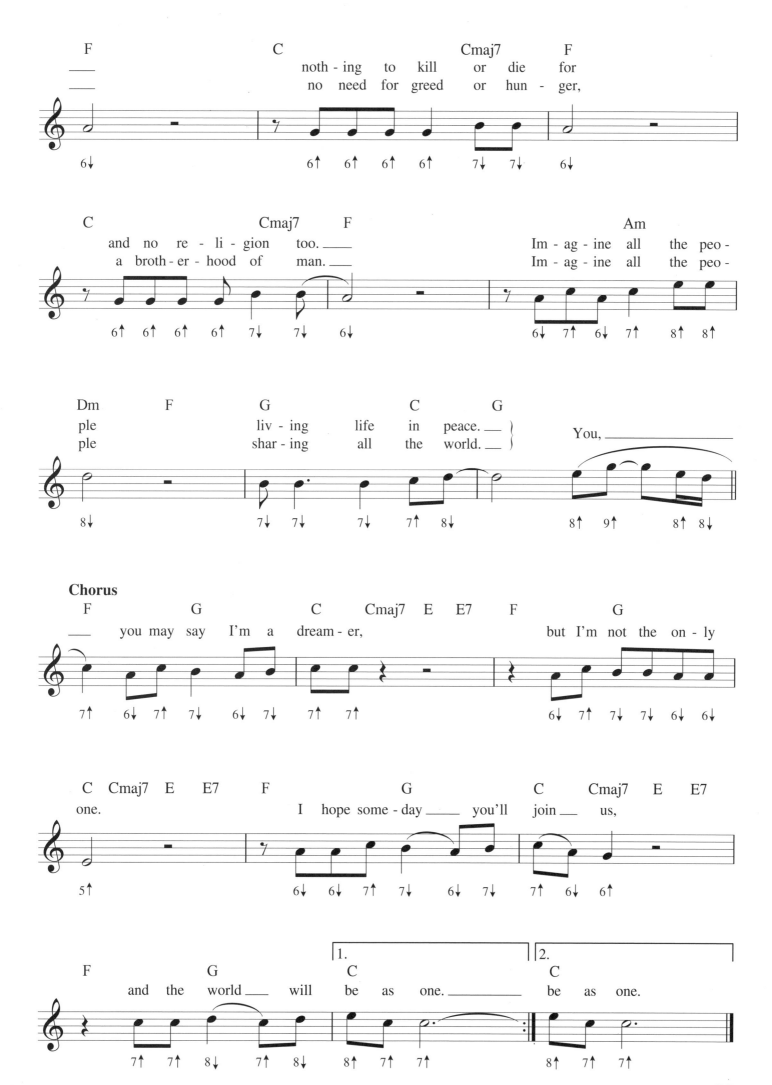

The Last Time I Saw Paris

from LADY, BE GOOD
Lyrics by Oscar Hammerstein II
Music by Jerome Kern

Verse
Moderately

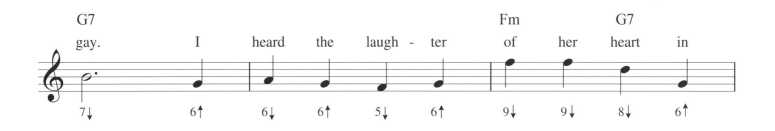

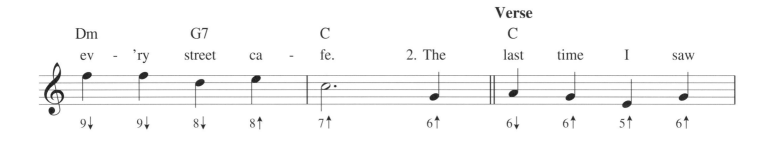

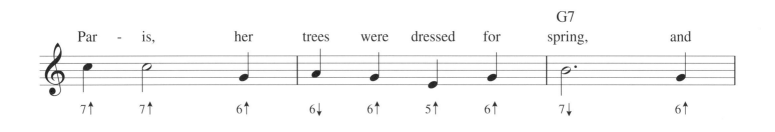

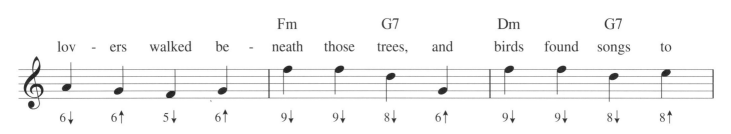

*Song sounds one octave higher than written.

Bridge

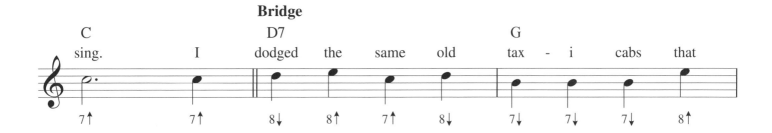

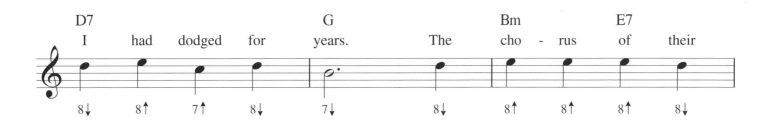

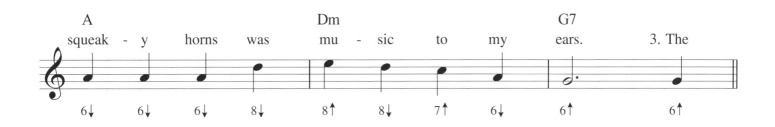

Verse

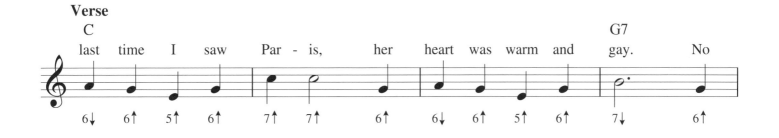

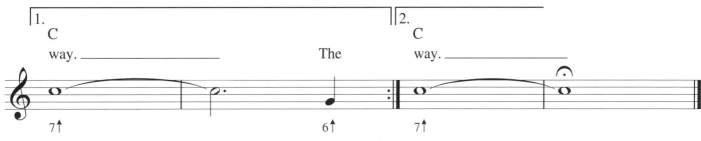

Let It Be

Words and Music by John Lennon and Paul McCartney

Verse
Slowly

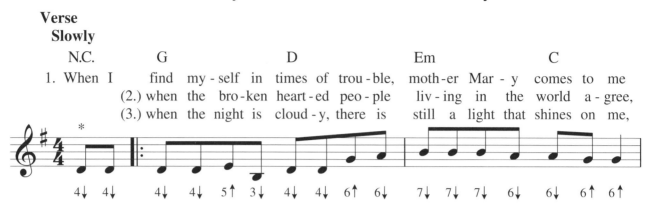

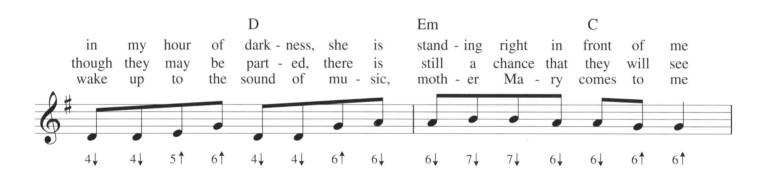

*Song sounds one octave higher than written.

Chorus

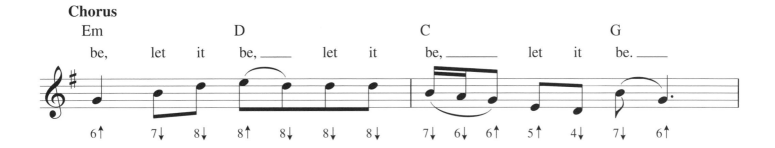

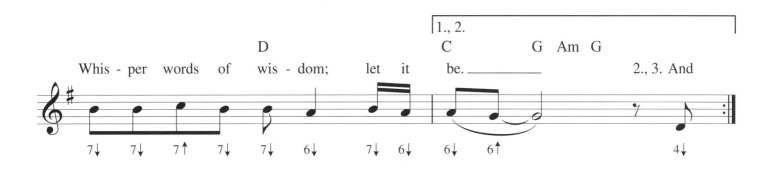

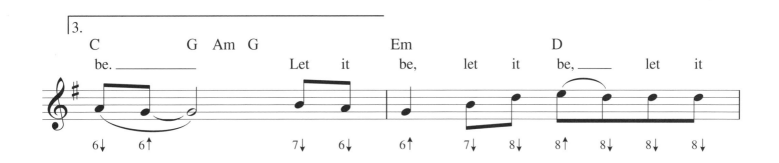

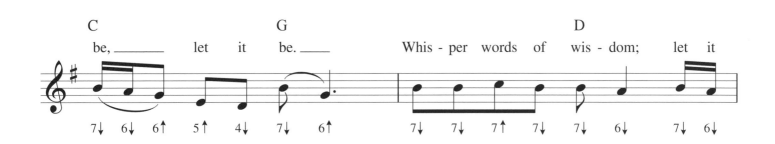

Outro

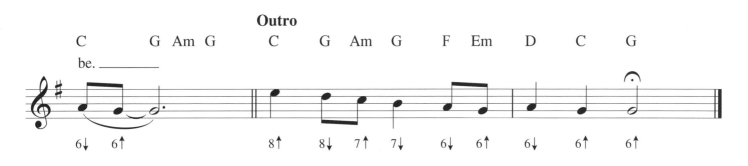

Love Me Tender

Words and Music by Elvis Presley and Vera Matson

Verse
Slowly

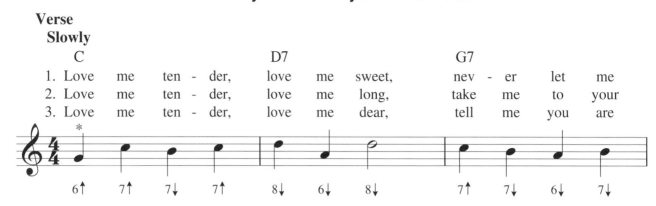

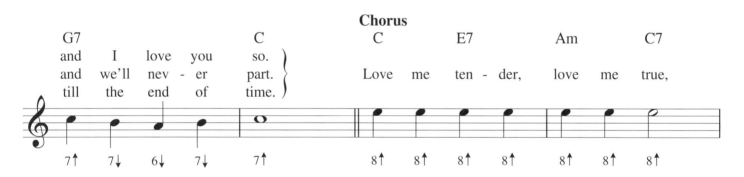

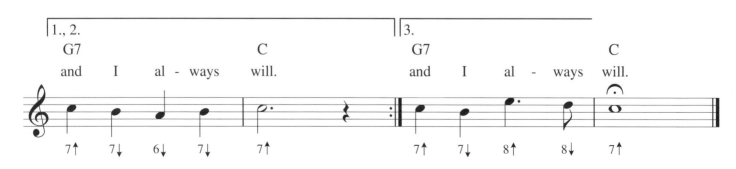

*Song sounds one octave higher than written.

My Heart Will Go On
(Love Theme From 'Titanic')

from the Paramount and Twentieth Century Fox Motion Picture TITANIC
Music by James Horner
Lyric by Will Jennings

Verse
Moderately

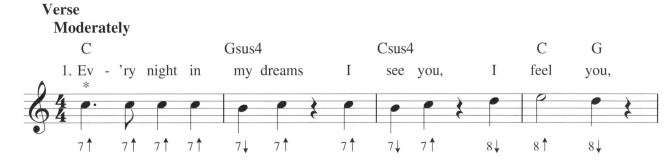

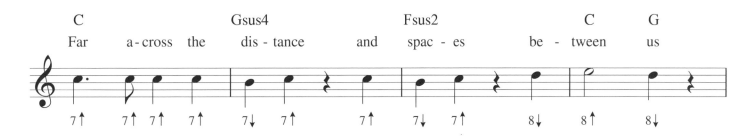

𝄋 Chorus

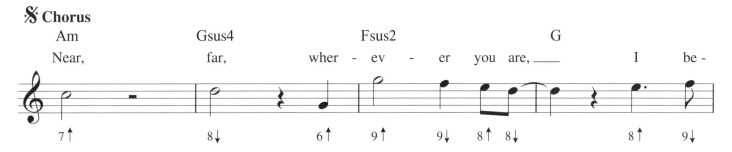

*Song sounds one octave higher than written.

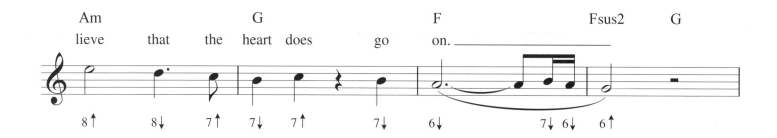

Am ..... G ..... F ..... Fsus2 ..... G

lieve that the heart does go on. _____

8↑ 8↓ 7↑ 7↓ 7↑ 7↓ 6↓ 7↓ 6↓ 6↑

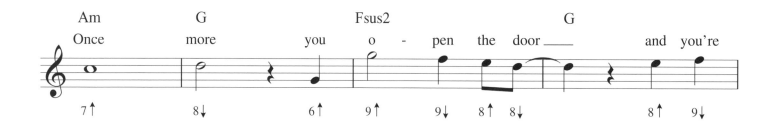

Am ..... G ..... Fsus2 ..... G

Once more you o - pen the door _____ and you're

7↑ 8↓ 6↑ 9↑ 9↓ 8↑ 8↓ 8↑ 9↓

To Coda ⊕

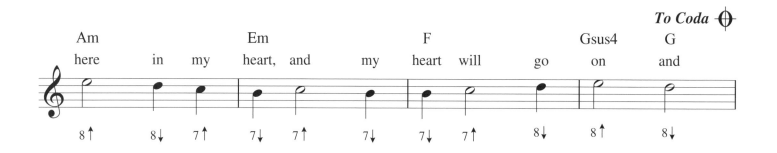

Am ..... Em ..... F ..... Gsus4 ..... G

here in my heart, and my heart will go on and

8↑ 8↓ 7↑ 7↓ 7↑ 7↓ 7↓ 7↑ 8↓ 8↑ 8↓

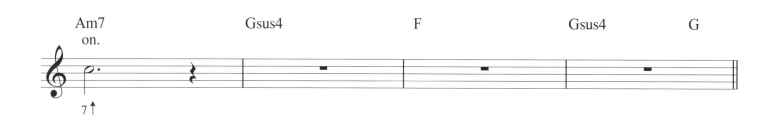

Am7 ..... Gsus4 ..... F ..... Gsus4 ..... G

on.

7↑

Verse

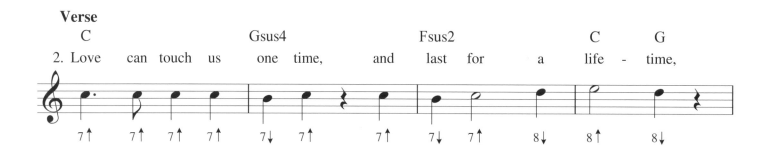

C ..... Gsus4 ..... Fsus2 ..... C ..... G

2. Love can touch us one time, and last for a life - time,

7↑ 7↑ 7↑ 7↑ 7↓ 7↑ 7↑ 7↓ 7↑ 8↓ 8↑ 8↓

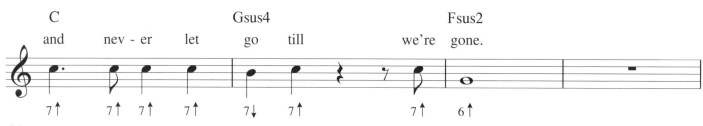

C ..... Gsus4 ..... Fsus2

and nev - er let go till we're gone.

7↑ 7↑ 7↑ 7↑ 7↓ 7↑ 7↑ 6↑

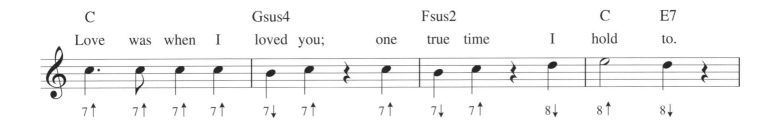

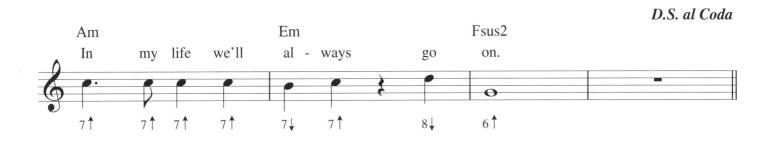

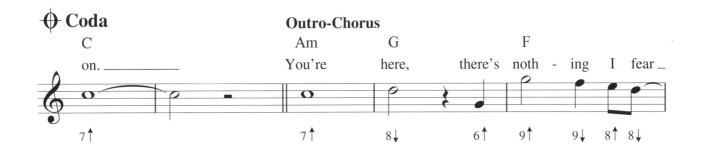

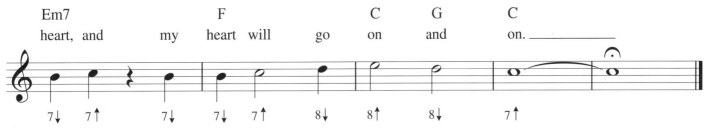

Maggie May

Words and Music by Rod Stewart and Martin Quittenton

*Song sounds one octave higher than written.

Chorus

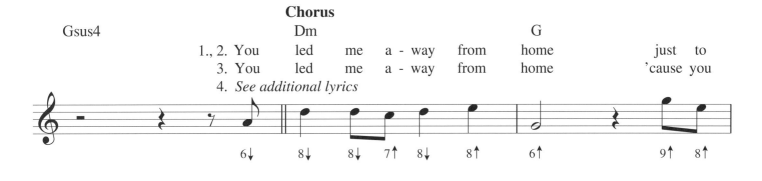

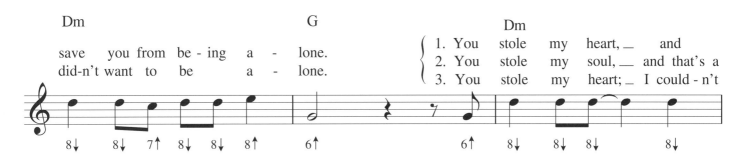

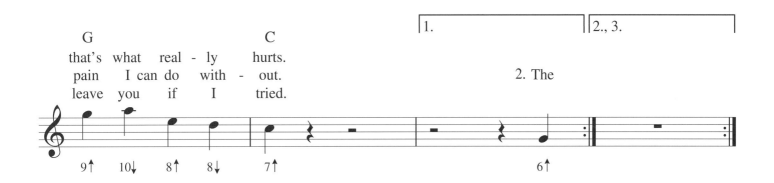

Outro

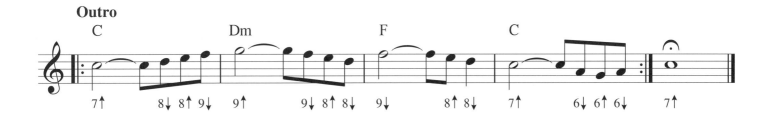

Additional Lyrics

3. All I needed was a friend to lend a guiding hand.
But you turned into a lover and mother, what a lover! You wore me out.
All you did was wreck my bed and in the morning kick me in the head.
Oh, Maggie, I couldn't have tried anymore.

4. I suppose I could collect my books and get on back to school,
Or steal my daddy's cue and make a living out of playing pool,
Or find myself a rock 'n' roll band that needs a helping hand.
Oh, Maggie, I wish I'd never seen your face.

Chorus 4. You made a first-class fool out of me.
But I'm as blind as a fool can be.
You stole me heart, but I love you anyway.

Moon River

from the Paramount Picture BREAKFAST AT TIFFANY'S
Words by Johnny Mercer
Music by Henry Mancini

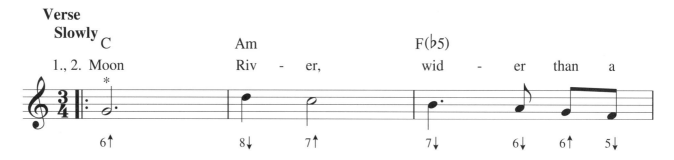

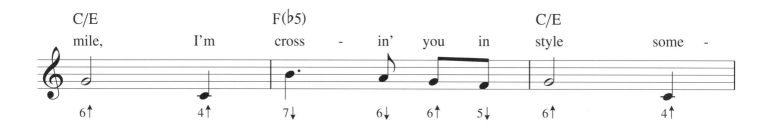

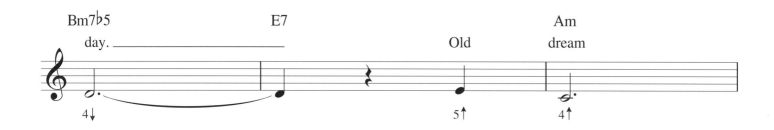

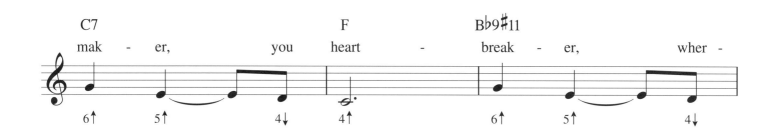

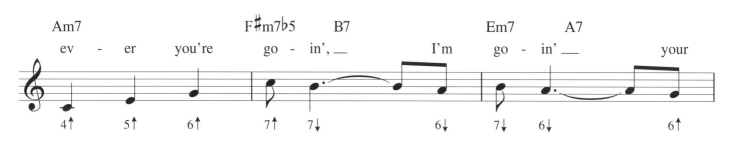

*Song sounds one octave higher than written.

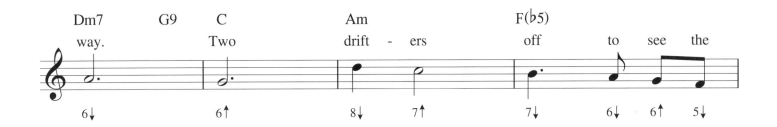

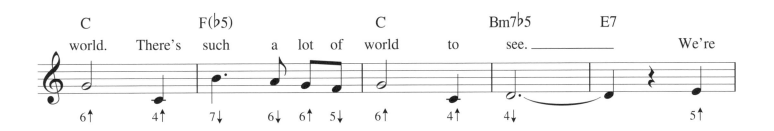

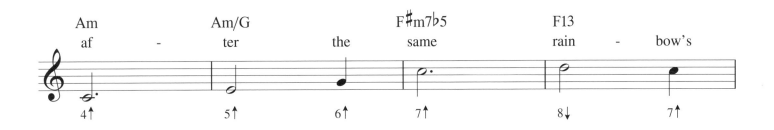

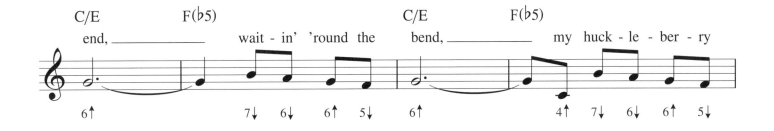

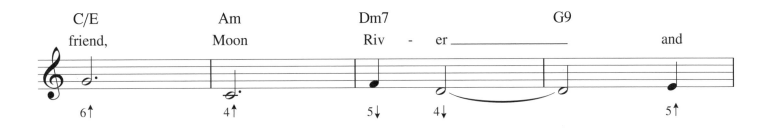

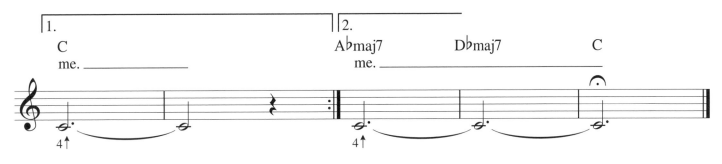

My Blue Heaven

Lyric by George Whiting
Music by Walter Donaldson

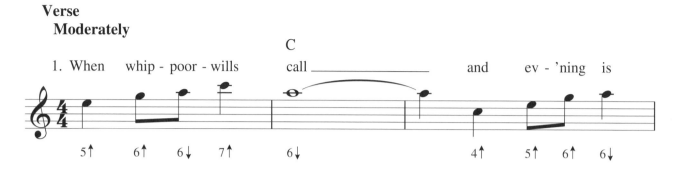

Verse
Moderately

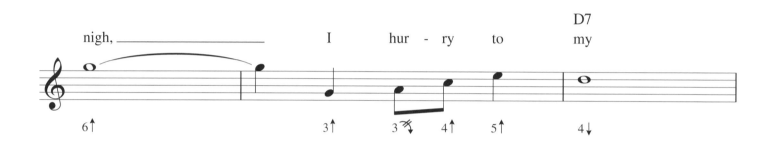

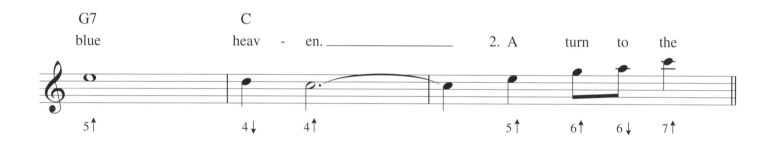

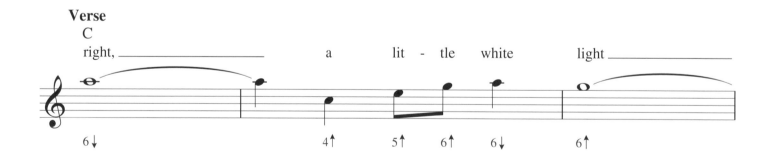

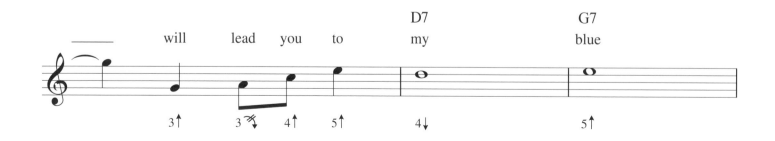

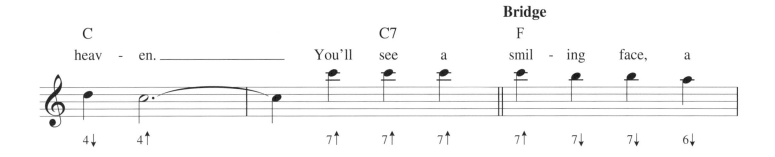

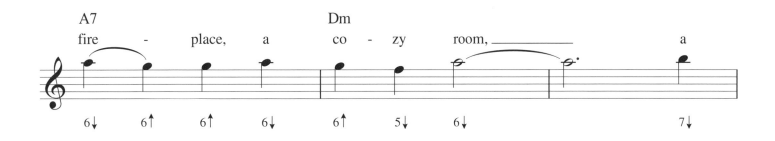

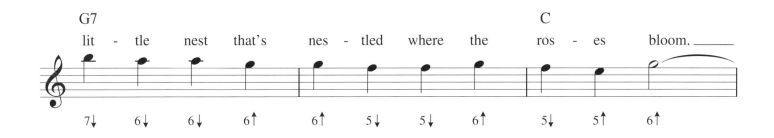

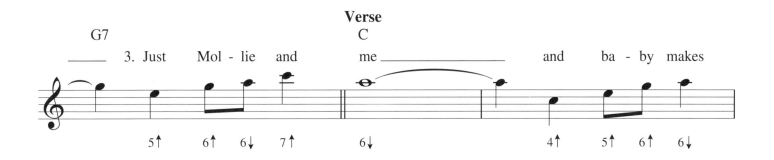

Verse

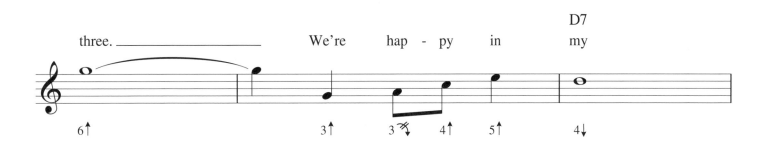

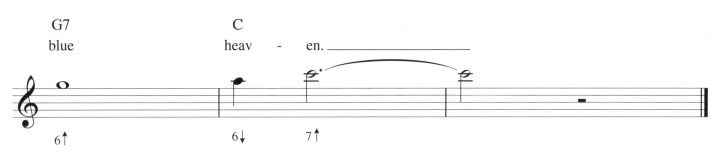

My Funny Valentine

from BABES IN ARMS
Words by Lorenz Hart
Music by Richard Rodgers

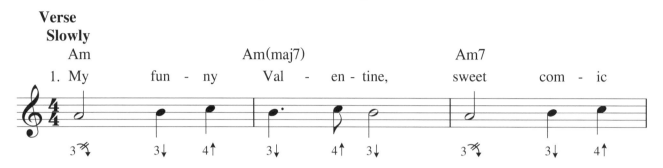

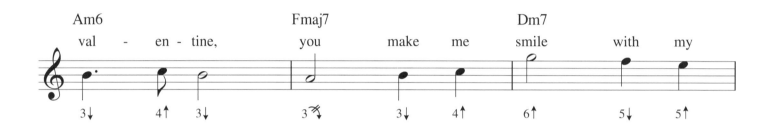

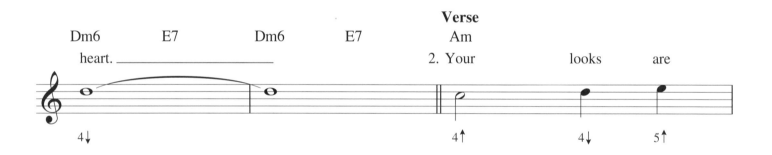

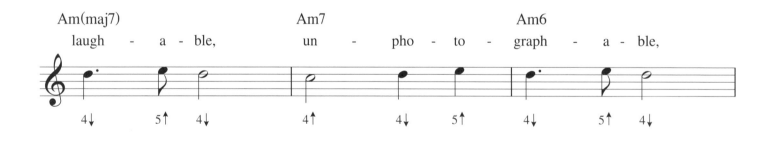

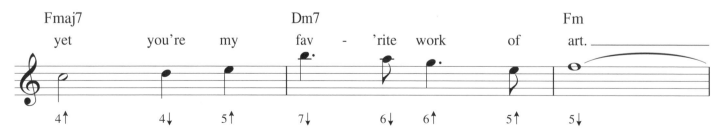

Bridge

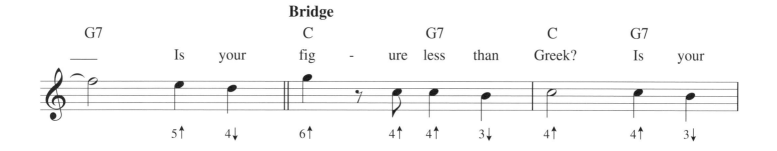

G7   C   G7   C   G7

___ Is your fig - ure less than Greek? Is your

5↑ 4↓ 6↑ 4↑ 4↑ 3↓ 4↑ 4↑ 3↓

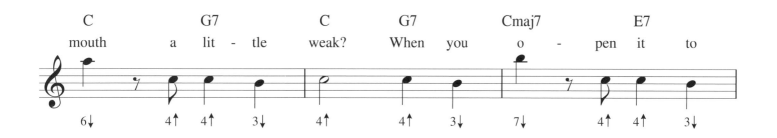

C   G7   C   G7   Cmaj7   E7

mouth a lit - tle weak? When you o - pen it to

6↓ 4↑ 4↑ 3↓ 4↑ 4↑ 3↓ 7↓ 4↑ 4↑ 3↓

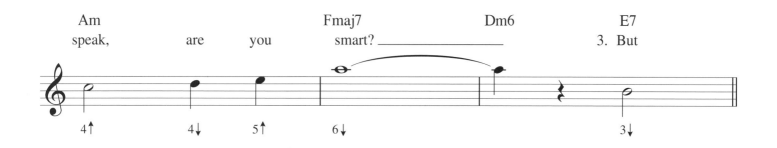

Am   Fmaj7   Dm6   E7

speak, are you smart? _____ 3. But

4↑ 4↓ 5↑ 6↓ 3↓

Verse

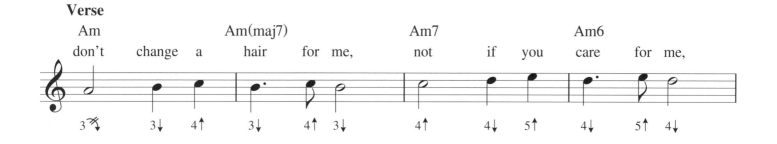

Am   Am(maj7)   Am7   Am6

don't change a hair for me, not if you care for me,

3↘ 3↓ 4↑ 3↓ 4↑ 3↓ 4↑ 4↓ 5↑ 4↓ 5↑ 4↓

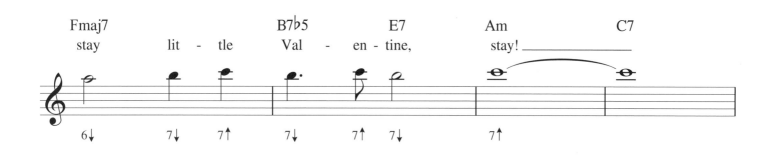

Fmaj7   B7♭5   E7   Am   C7

stay lit - tle Val - en - tine, stay! _____

6↓ 7↓ 7↑ 7↓ 7↑ 7↓ 7↑

Fmaj7   Dm7   G7   C

Each day is Val - en - tine's day. _____

4↑ 4↓ 5↑ 4↓ 5↑ 4↓ 4↑

My Girl

Words and Music by William "Smokey" Robinson and Ronald White

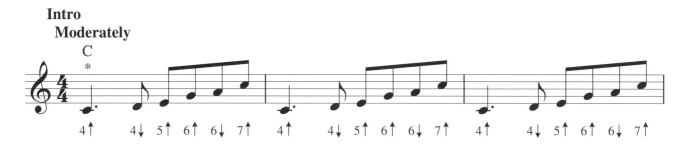

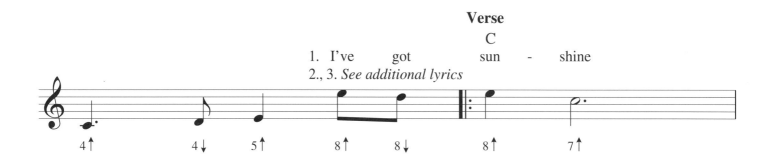

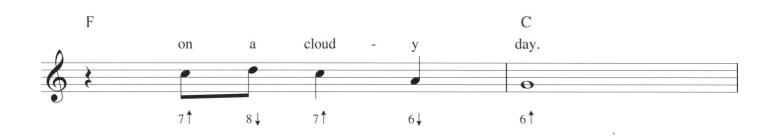

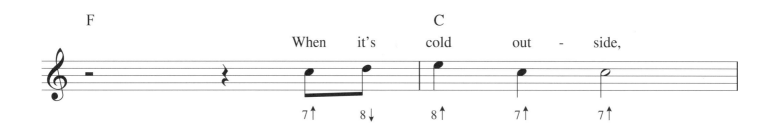

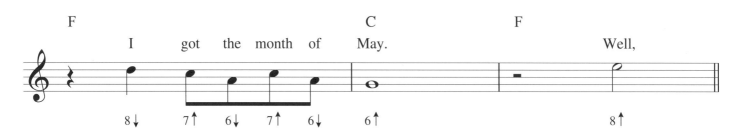

*Song sounds one octave higher than written.

Chorus

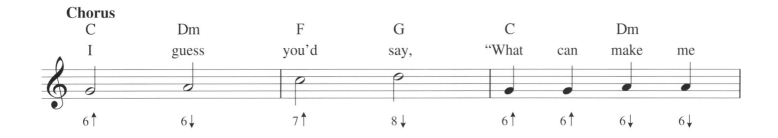

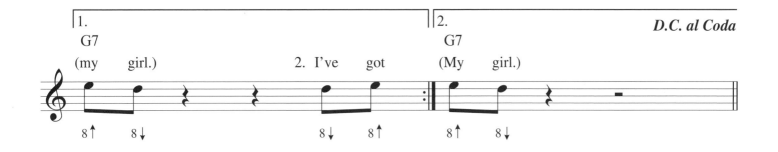

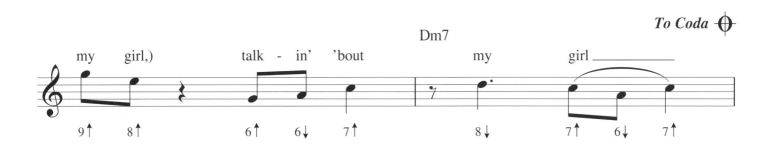

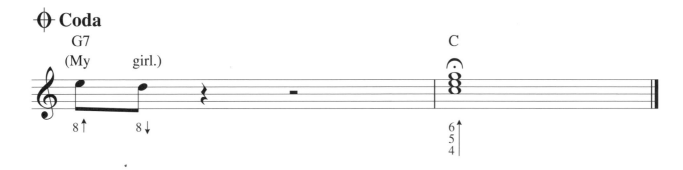

Additional Lyrics

2. I've got so much honey the bees envy me.
   I've got a sweeter song than the birds in the tree.

3. I don't need no money, fortune, or fame.
   I got all the riches, baby, one man can claim.

My Romance

from JUMBO
Words by Lorenz Hart
Music by Richard Rodgers

Intro
Moderately slow

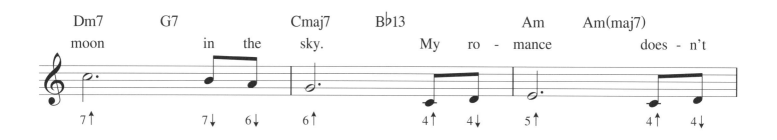

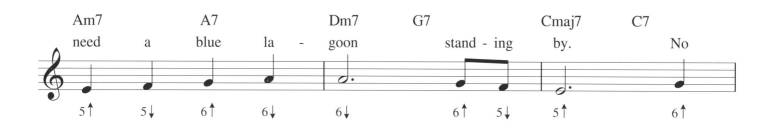

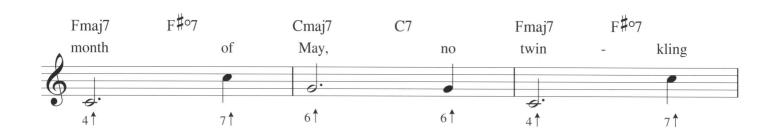

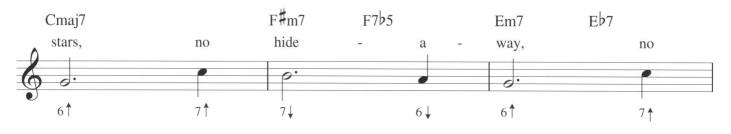

*Song sounds one octave higher than written.

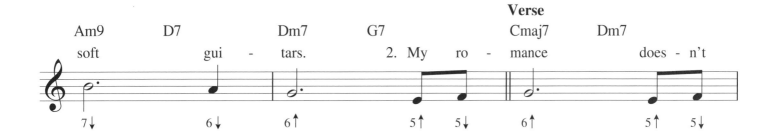

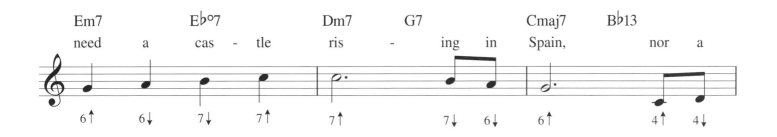

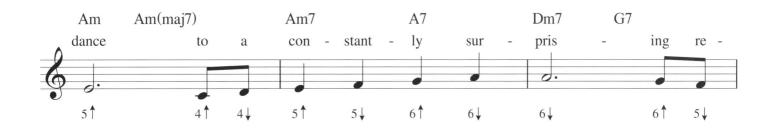

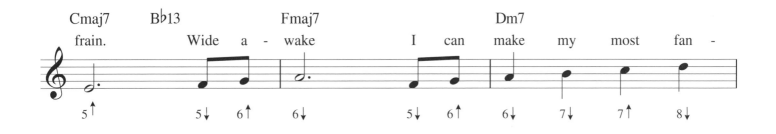

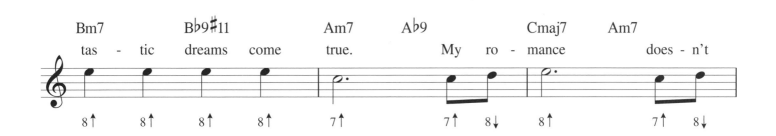

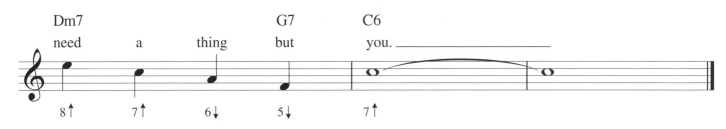

Nowhere Man

Words and Music by John Lennon and Paul McCartney

Verse
Moderately

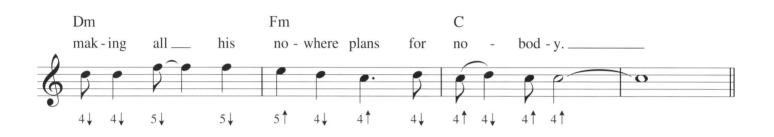

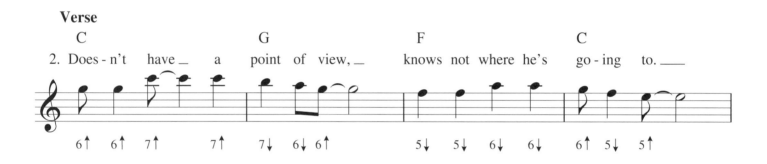

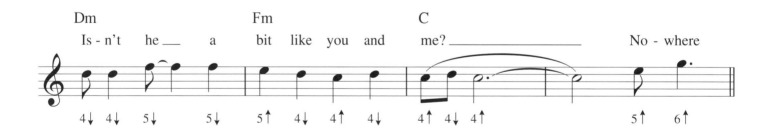

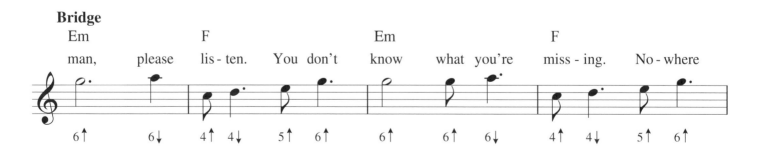

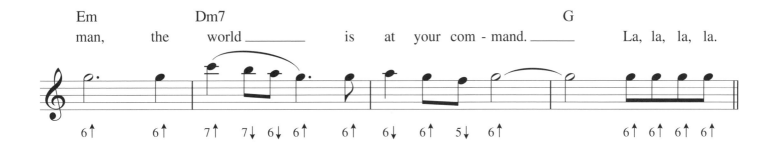

man,   the   world _____ is   at   your com - mand. _____   La, la, la, la.

Interlude

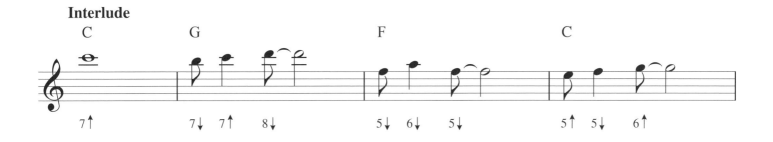

Verse

3. He's as blind as   he can be, __   just sees what he   wants to   see. __

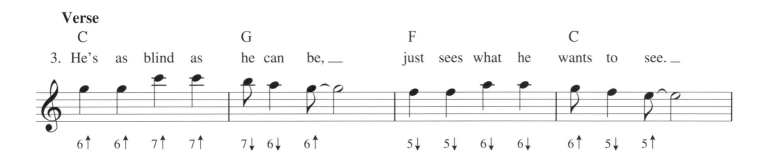

No - where man, __ can   you see me at   all? _____   No - where

Bridge

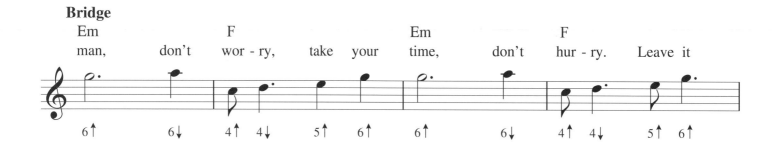

Em / man, don't / F wor - ry, take your / Em time, don't / F hur - ry. Leave it

6↑ 6↓ 4↑ 4↓ 5↑ 6↑ 6↑ 6↓ 4↑ 4↓ 5↑ 6↑

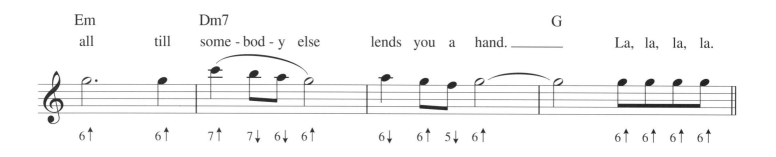

Em / all till Dm7 some - bod - y else lends you a hand. _____ G La, la, la, la.

6↑ 6↑ 7↑ 7↓ 6↓ 6↑ 6↓ 6↑ 5↓ 6↑ 6↑ 6↑ 6↑ 6↑

Verse

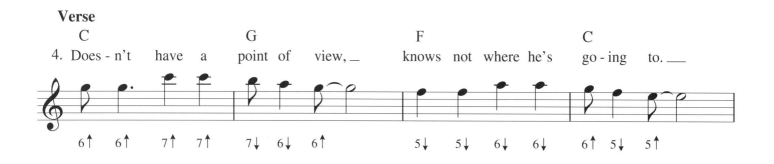

C / 4. Does - n't have a G point of view, __ F knows not where he's C go - ing to. __

6↑ 6↑ 7↑ 7↑ 7↓ 6↓ 6↑ 5↓ 5↓ 6↓ 6↓ 6↑ 5↓ 5↑

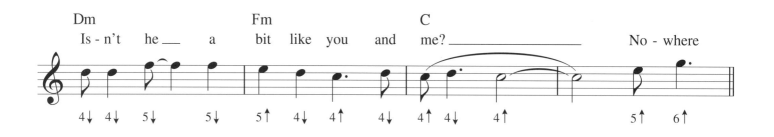

Dm / Is - n't he __ a Fm bit like you and me? C _____ No - where

4↓ 4↓ 5↓ 5↓ 5↑ 4↓ 4↑ 4↓ 4↑ 4↓ 4↑ 5↑ 6↑

Bridge

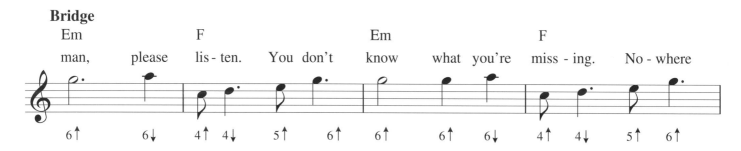

Em / man, please lis - ten. F You don't know Em what you're miss - ing. F No - where

6↑ 6↓ 4↑ 4↓ 5↑ 6↑ 6↑ 6↑ 6↓ 4↑ 4↓ 5↑ 6↑

62

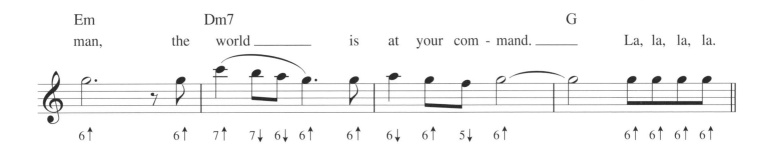

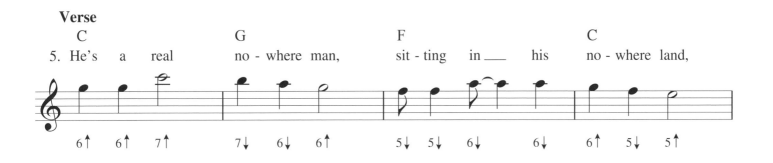

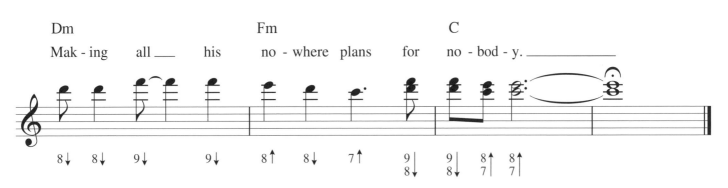

Piano Man

Words and Music by Billy Joel

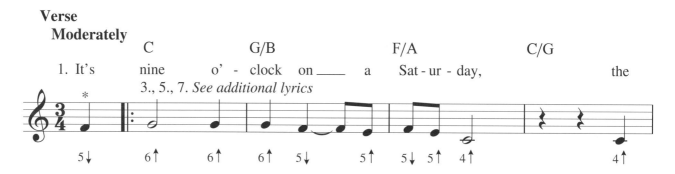

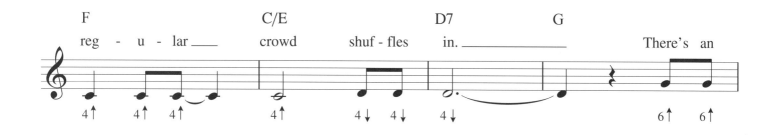

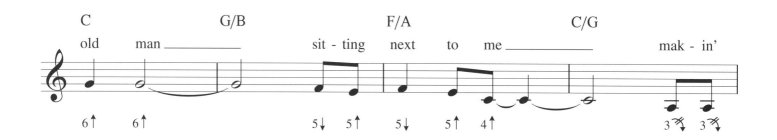

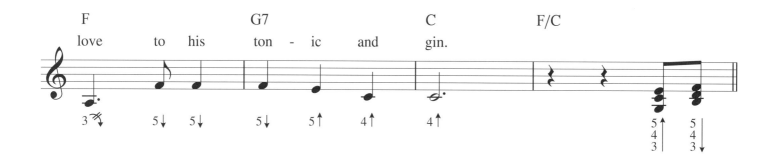

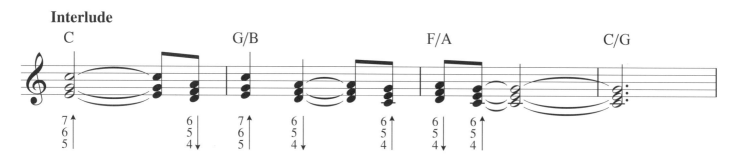

*Song sounds one octave higher than written.

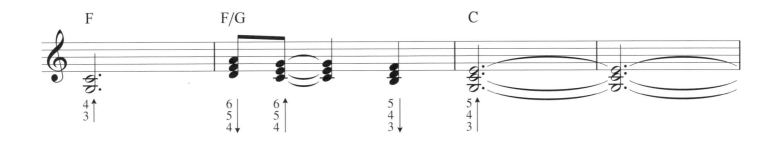

Verse

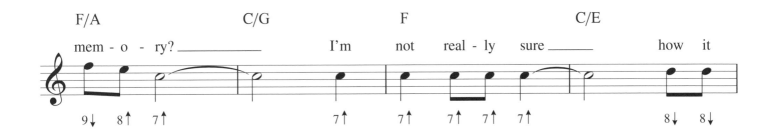

2. He says, "Son, can you play me _____ a
4., 6., 8. *See additional lyrics*

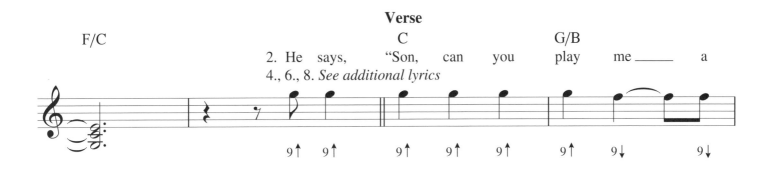

mem - o - ry? _____ I'm not real - ly sure _____ how it

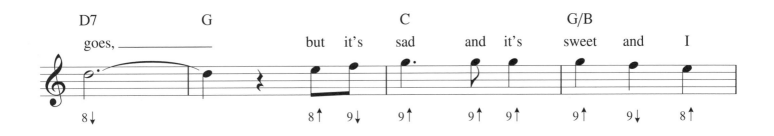

goes, _____ but it's sad and it's sweet and I

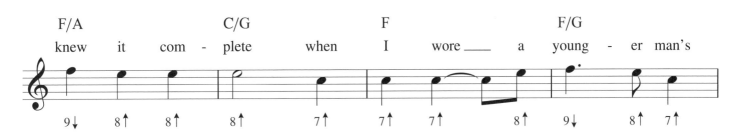

knew it com - plete when I wore _____ a young - er man's

Bridge

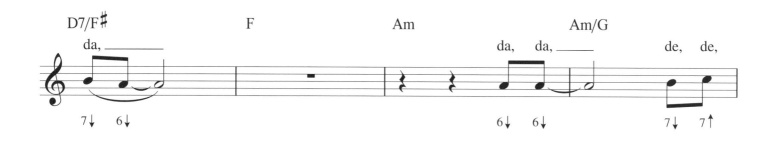

Chorus

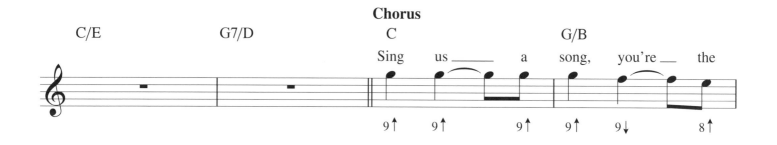

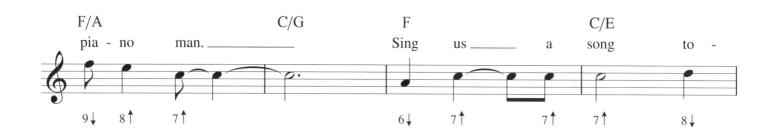

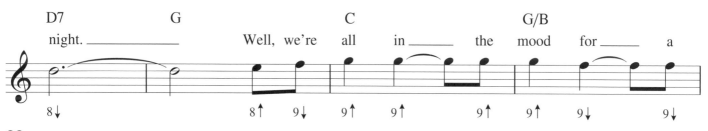

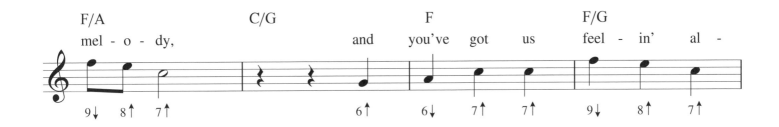

F/A   C/G   F   F/G

mel - o - dy,   and   you've   got   us   feel - in'   al -

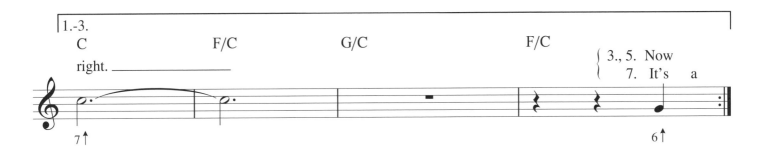

1.-3.

C   F/C   G/C   F/C

right. _____   3., 5. Now   7. It's   a

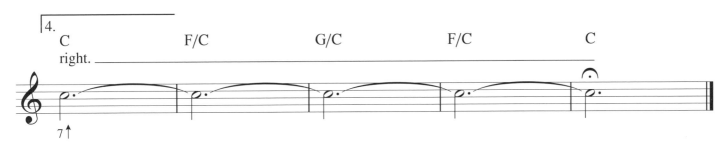

4.

C   F/C   G/C   F/C   C

right. _____

Additional Lyrics

3. Now John at the bar is a friend of mine,
   He gets me my drinks for free.
   And he's quick with a joke or to light up your smoke,
   But there's someplace that he'd rather be.

4. He says, "Bill, I believe this is killing me,"
   As the smile ran away from his face.
   "Well, I'm sure that I could be a movie star
   If I could get out of this place."

5. Now Paul is a real estate novelist,
   Who never had time for a wife.
   And he's talking with Davy, who's still in the Navy,
   And probably will be for life.

6. And the waitress is practicing politics,
   As the businessmen slowly get stoned.
   Yes, they're sharing a drink they call loneliness,
   But it's better than drinkin' alone.

7. It's a pretty good crowd for a Saturday,
   And the manager gives me a smile.
   'Cause he knows that it's me they've been comin' to see
   To forget about life for a while.

8. And the piano sounds like a carnival,
   And the microphone smells like a beer.
   And they sit at the bar, and put bread in my jar,
   And say, "Man, what are you doin' here?"

Raindrops Keep Fallin' on My Head

Lyric by Hal David
Music by Burt Bacharach

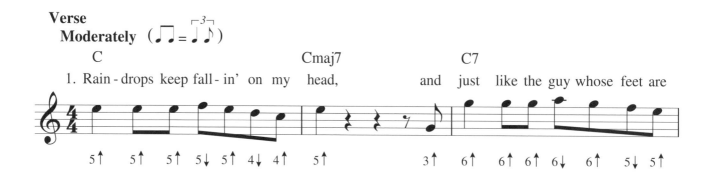

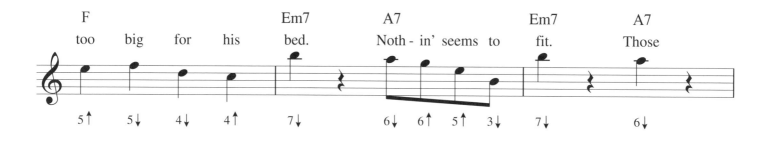

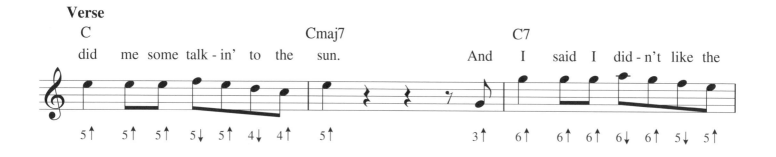

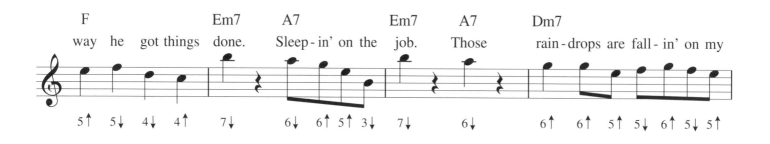

Rainy Days and Mondays

Lyrics by Paul Williams
Music by Roger Nichols

Intro
Moderately slow

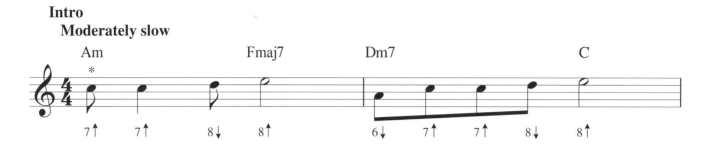

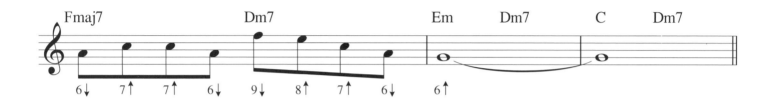

Verse

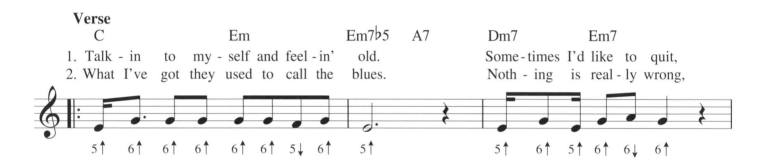

1. Talk - in   to my - self and feel - in'   old.   Some - times I'd like to   quit,
2. What I've got they used to call the   blues.   Noth - ing   is real - ly wrong,

noth - in' ev - er seems to   fit.   Hang - in'   a - round,
feel - in like I don't be - long.   Walk - in'   a - round,

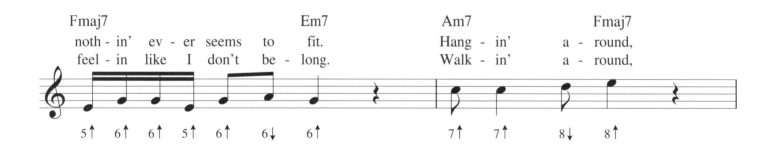

noth - in' to do   but frown. }   Rain - y days and Mon - days   al - ways get me
some kind   of lone - ly clown. }

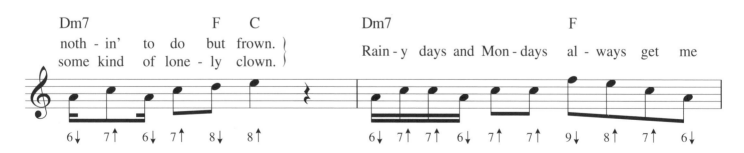

*Song sounds one octave higher than written.

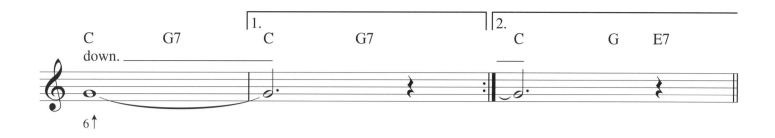

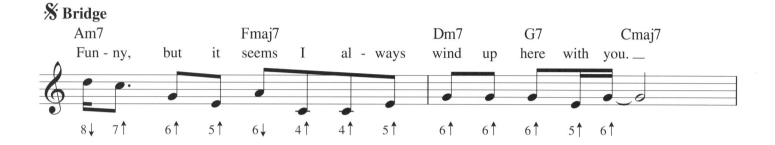

𝄋 Bridge

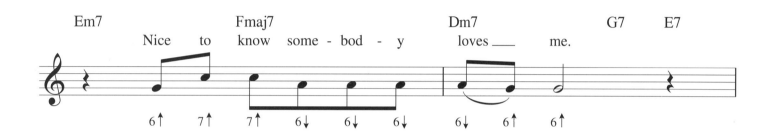

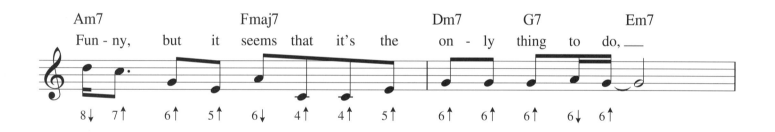

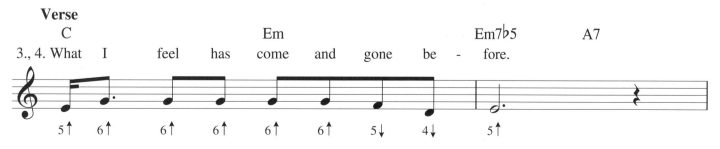

Verse

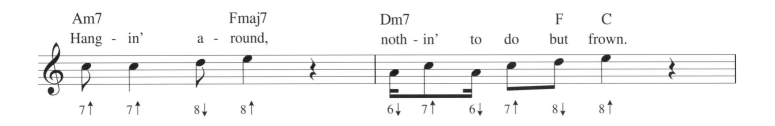

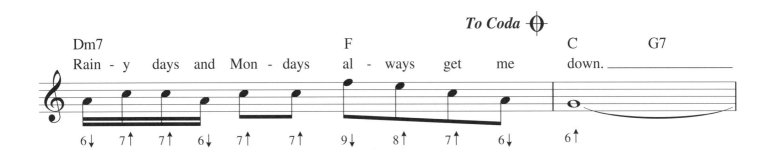

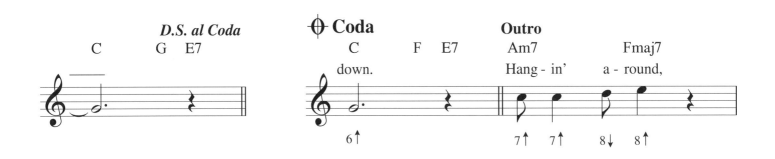

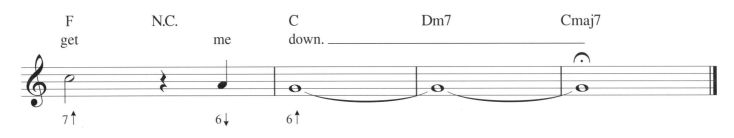

Time in a Bottle

Words and Music by Jim Croce

Verse
Moderately

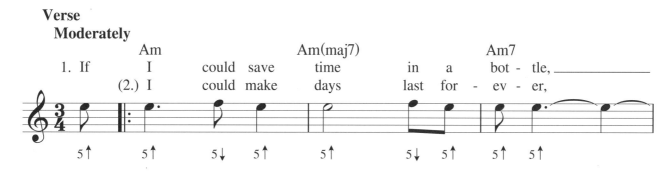

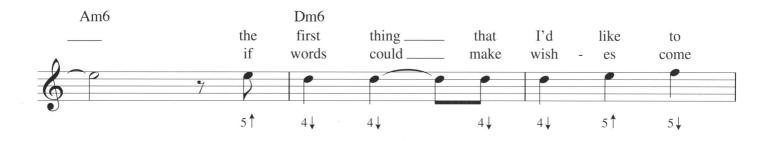

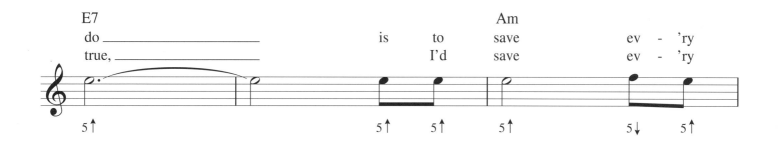

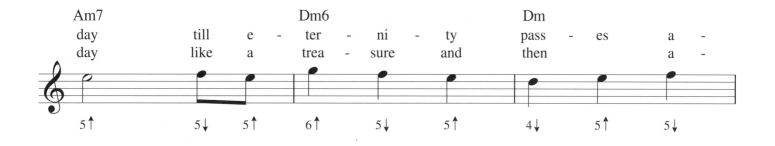

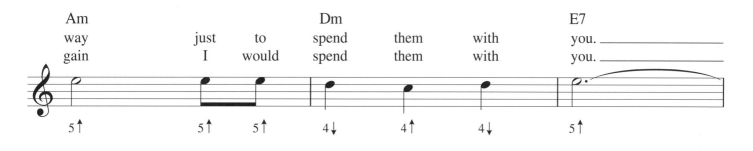

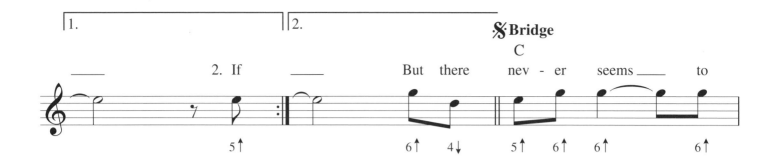

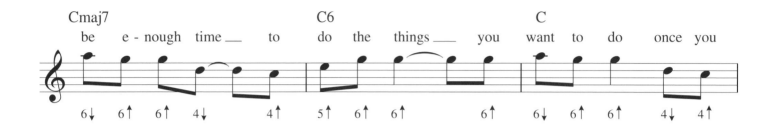

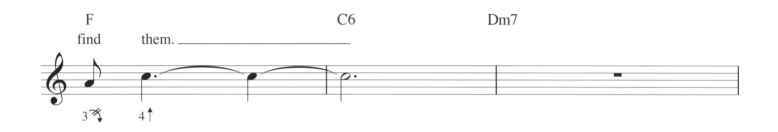

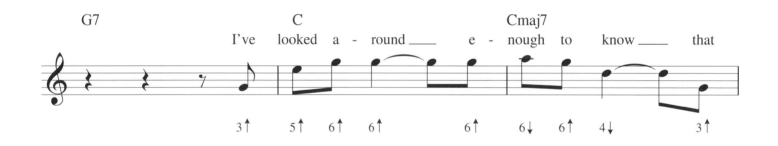

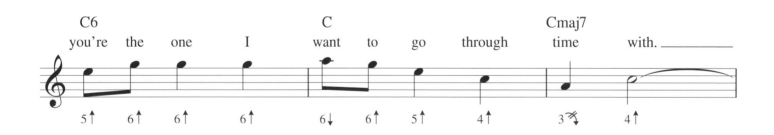

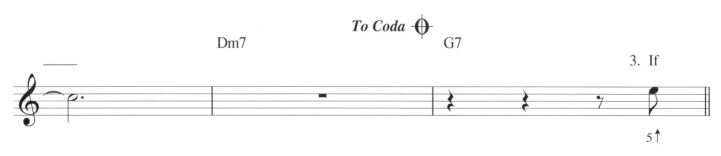

Verse

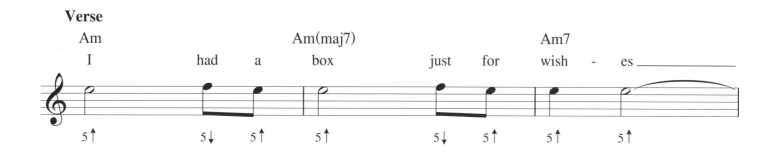

Am
I   had   a   box   just   for   wish - es _____

5↑   5↓ 5↑   5↑   5↓ 5↑   5↑   5↑

Am(maj7)

Am7

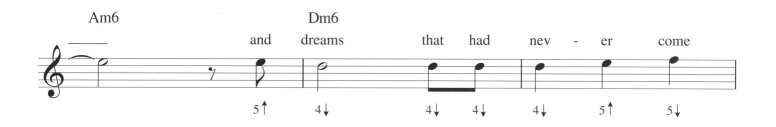

Am6
_____   and   dreams   that   had   nev - er   come

5↑   4↓   4↓   4↓   4↓   5↑   5↓

Dm6

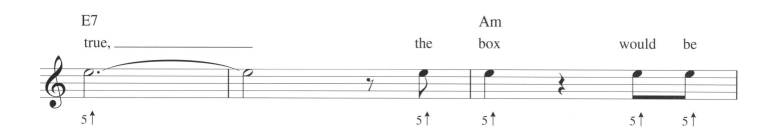

E7
true, _____   the   box   would   be

5↑   5↑   5↑   5↑   5↑

Am

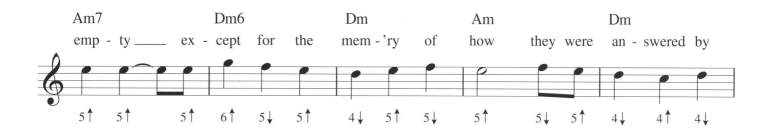

Am7
emp - ty ___ ex - cept   for   the   mem -'ry   of   how   they   were   an - swered   by

5↑   5↑   5↑   6↑   5↓   5↑   4↓   5↑   5↓   5↑   5↓   5↑   4↓   4↑   4↓

Dm6   Dm   Am   Dm

D.S. al Coda

⊕ **Coda**

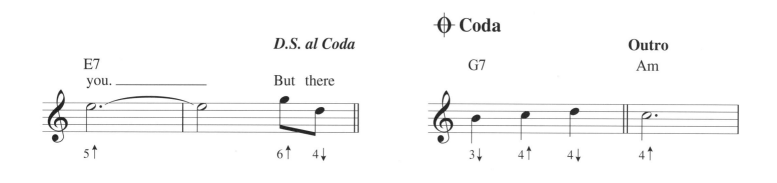

E7
you. _____   But   there

5↑   6↑   4↓

Outro
G7   Am

3↓   4↑   4↓   4↑

3↓   4↑   4↓   4↑   3↓   4↑   4↓   6↓
rit.

Stand by Me

Words and Music by Jerry Leiber, Mike Stoller and Ben E. King

*Song sounds one octave higher than written.

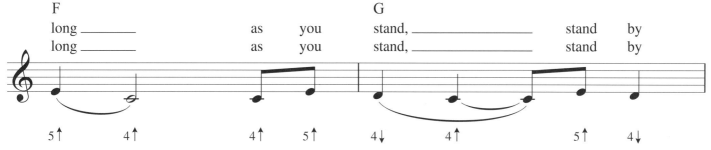

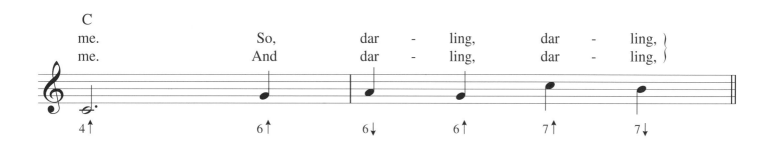

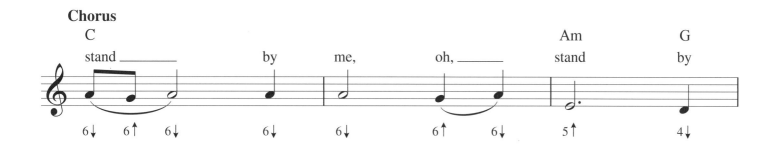

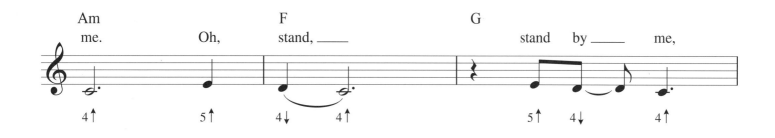

Chorus

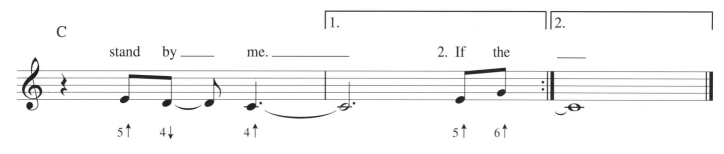

77

A Time for Us
(Love Theme)

from the Paramount Picture ROMEO AND JULIET
Words by Larry Kusik and Eddie Snyder
Music by Nino Rota

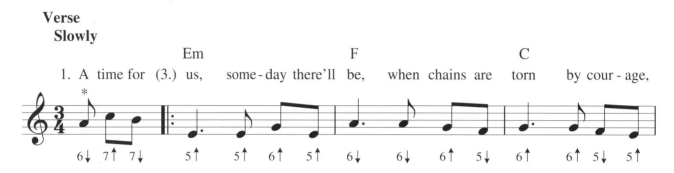

Verse
Slowly

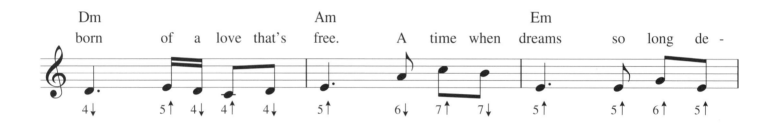

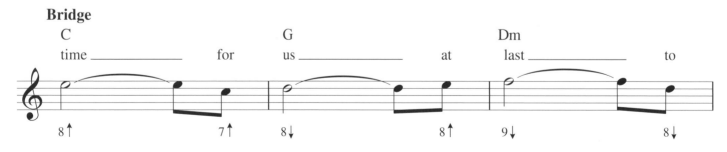

*Song sounds one octave higher than written.

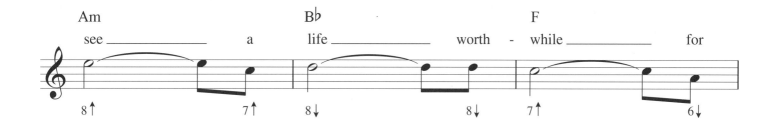

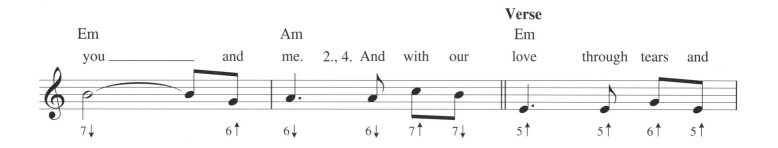

Verse

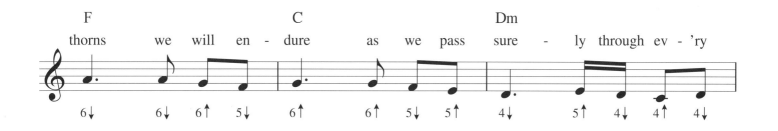

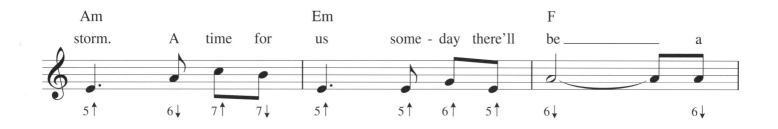

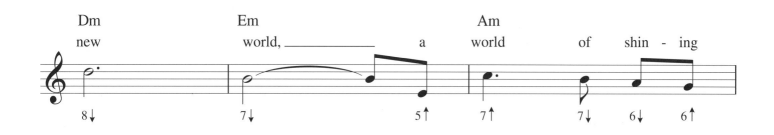

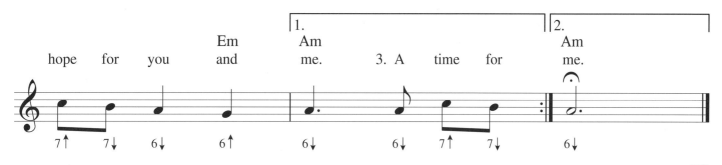

Unchained Melody

Lyric by Hy Zaret
Music by Alex North

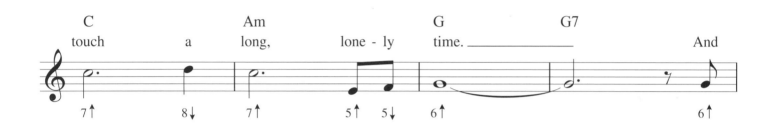

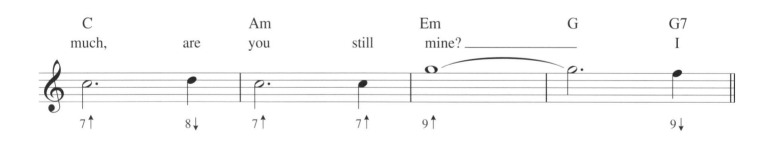

*Song sounds one octave higher than written.

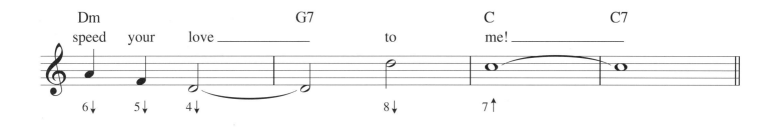

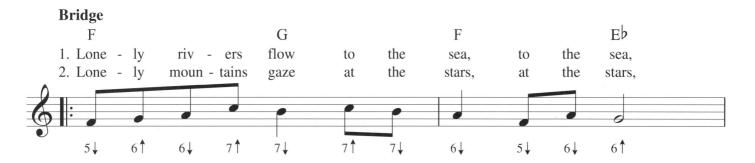

Bridge

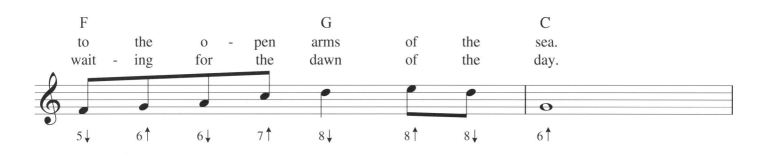

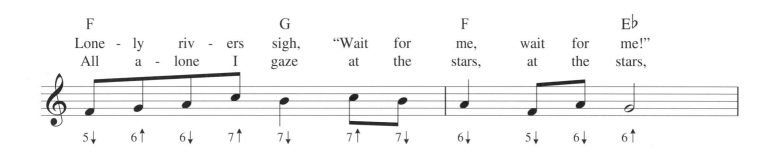

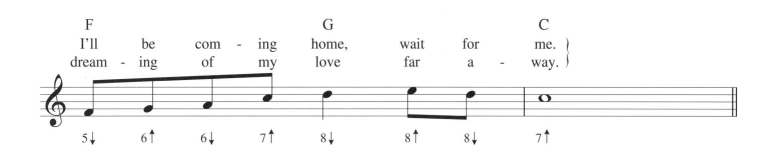

Verse

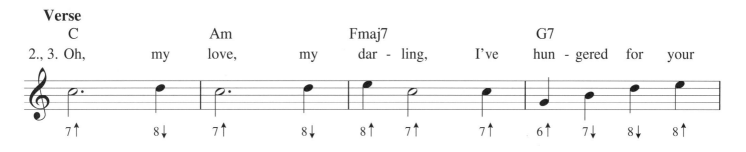

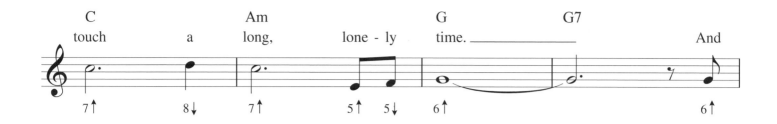

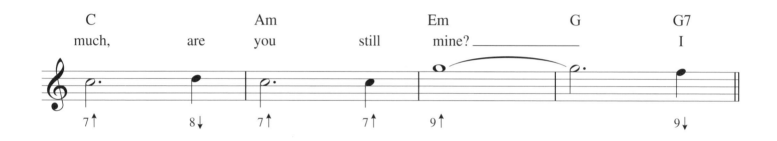

Chorus

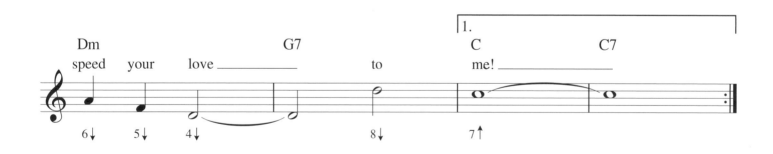

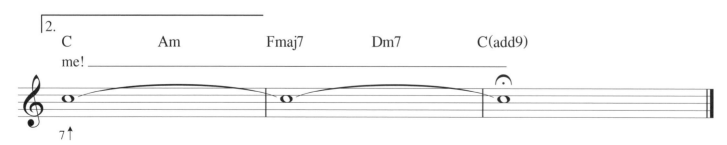

We Will Rock You

Words and Music by Brian May

Verse
Moderate Rock

N.C.

1. Bud - dy you're a boy, make a big noise play - in' in the
2. Bud - dy you're a young man, hard man shout - in' in the
3. Bud - dy you're an old man, poor man plead - in' with your

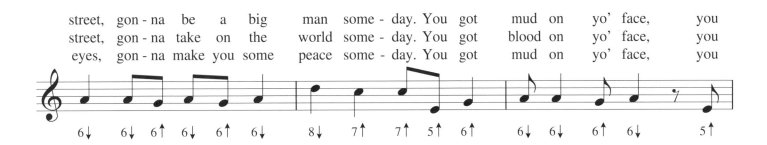

6↑ 6↓ 6↓ 6↑ 6↓ 6↓ 6↑ 6↓ 6↓ 6↑ 6↓ 6↓ 6↑

street, gon - na be a big man some - day. You got mud on yo' face, you
street, gon - na take on the world some - day. You got blood on yo' face, you
eyes, gon - na make you some peace some - day. You got mud on yo' face, you

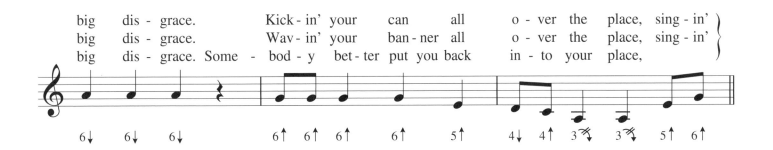

6↓ 6↓ 6↑ 6↓ 6↑ 6↓ 8↓ 7↑ 7↑ 5↑ 6↑ 6↓ 6↓ 6↑ 6↓ 5↑

big dis - grace. Kick - in' your can all o - ver the place, sing - in'
big dis - grace. Wav - in' your ban - ner all o - ver the place, sing - in'
big dis - grace. Some - bod - y bet - ter put you back in - to your place,

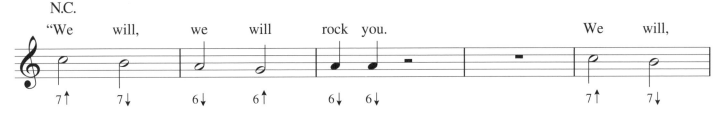

6↓ 6↓ 6↓ 6↑ 6↑ 6↑ 6↑ 5↑ 4↓ 4↑ 3⤨ 3⤨ 5↑ 6↑

Chorus

N.C.

"We will, we will rock you. We will,

7↑ 7↓ 6↓ 6↑ 6↓ 6↓ 7↑ 7↓

1., 2. we will rock you." **3.** rock you."

6↓ 6↑ 6↓ 6↓ 6↓ 6↓

*Song sounds one octave higher than written.

What the World Needs Now Is Love

Lyric by Hal David
Music by Burt Bacharach

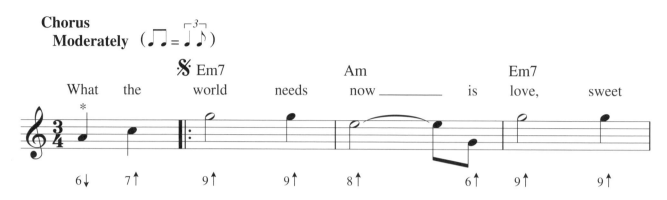

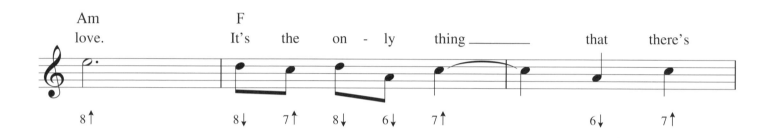

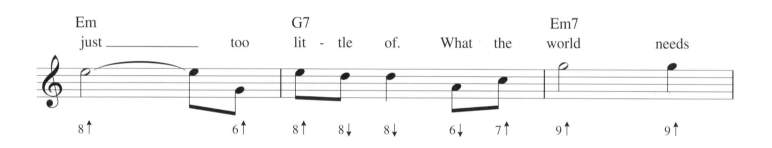

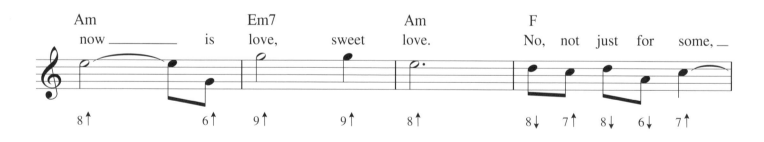

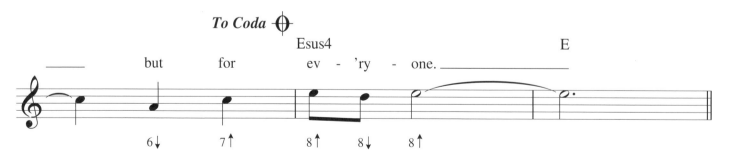

*Song sounds one octave higher than written.

When I Fall in Love

Words by Edward Heyman
Music by Victor Young

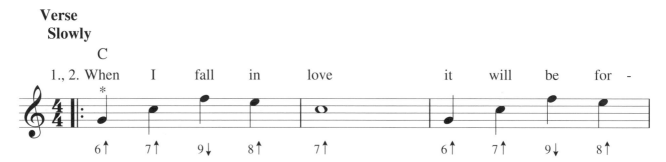

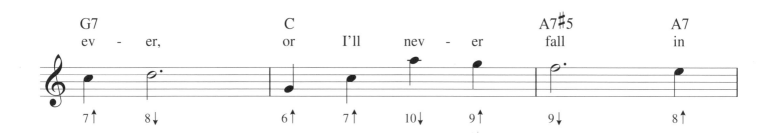

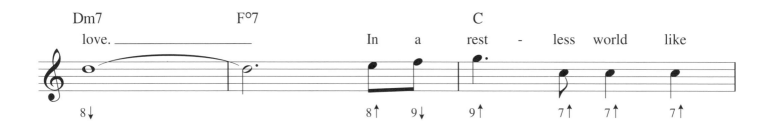

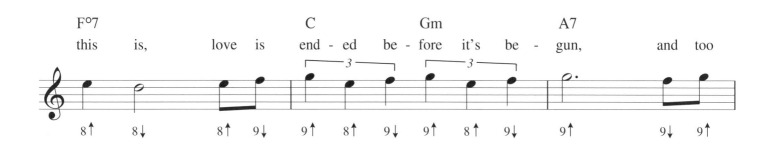

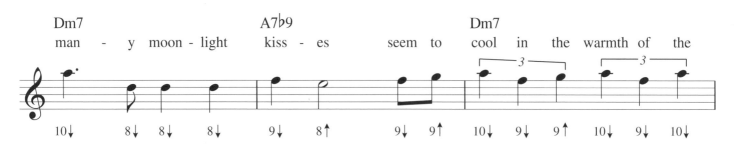

*Song sounds one octave higher than written.

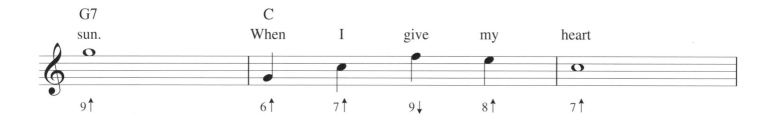

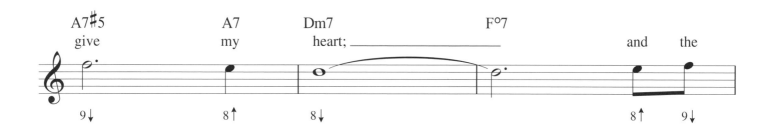

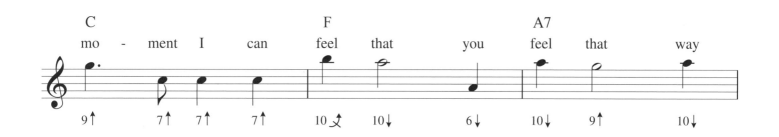

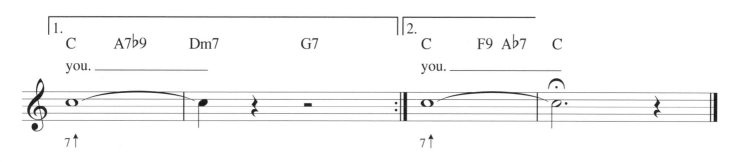

With a Little Help from My Friends

Words and Music by John Lennon and Paul McCartney

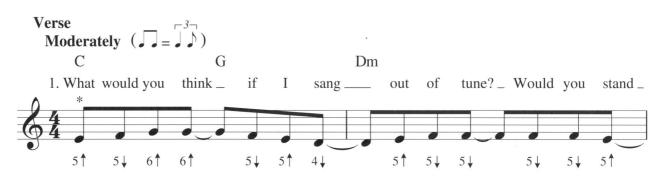

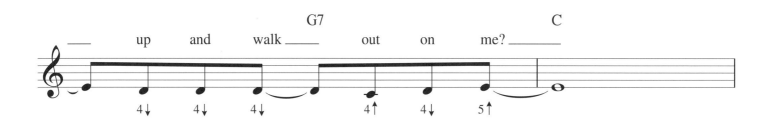

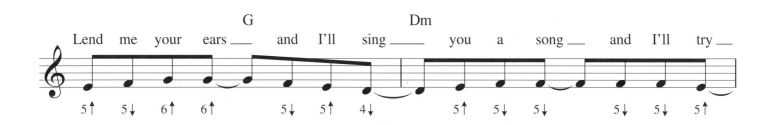

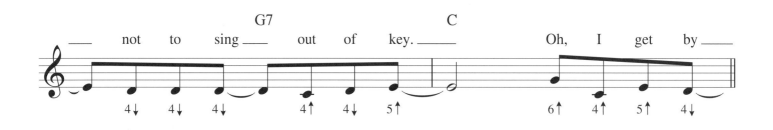

Chorus

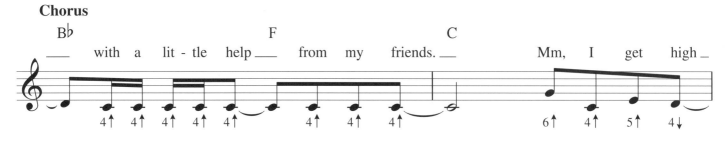

*Song sounds one octave higher than written.

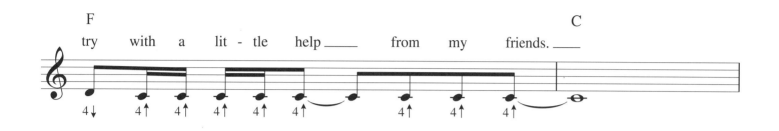

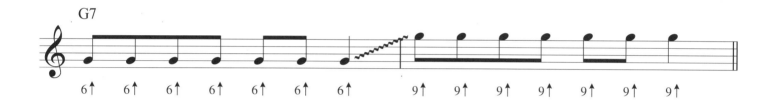

Verse

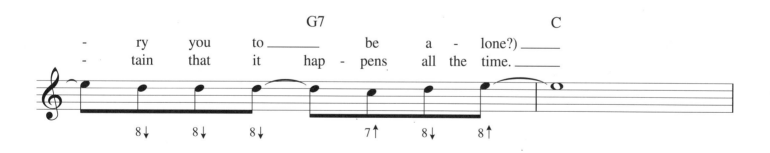

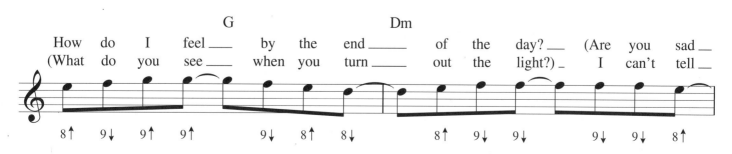

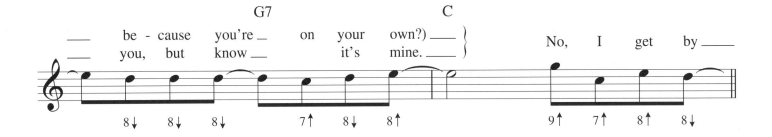

Chorus

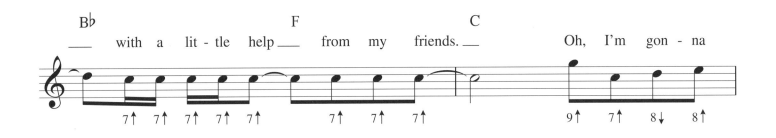

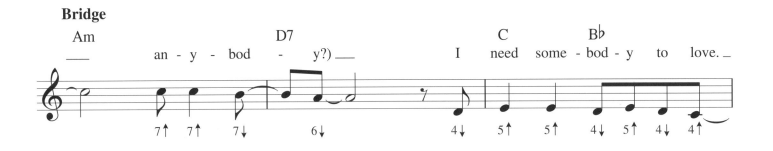

Bridge

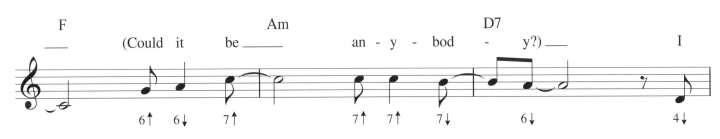

90

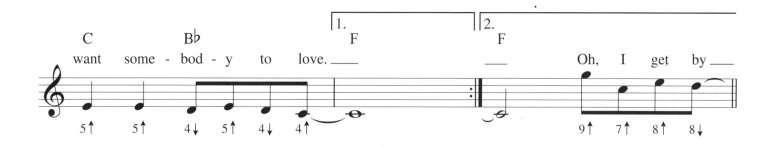

Outro

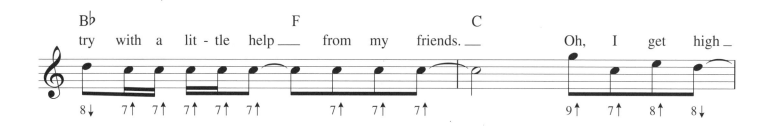

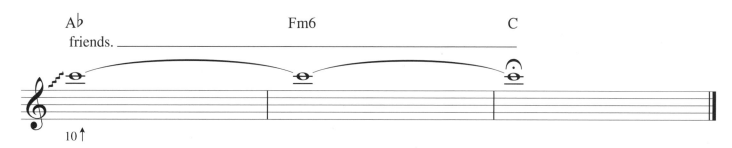

Yellow Submarine

Words and Music by John Lennon and Paul McCartney

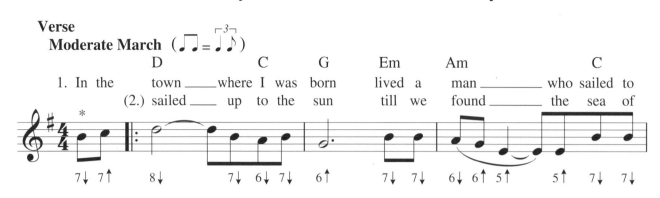

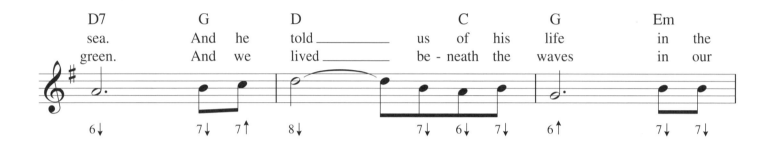

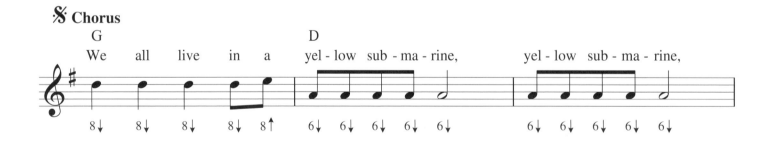

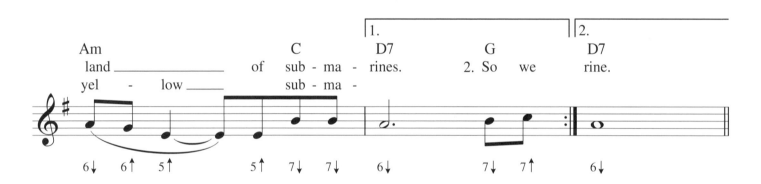

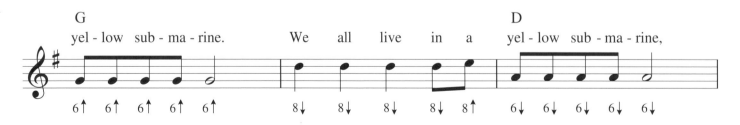

*Song sounds one octave higher than written.

You Are My Sunshine

Words and Music by Jimmie Davis

Verse
Moderately

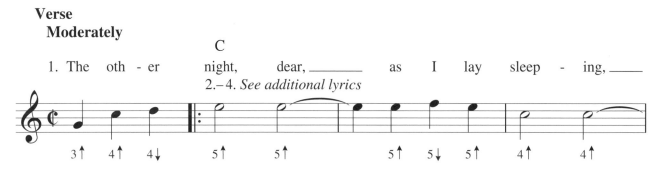

1. The oth - er night, dear, _____ as I lay sleep - ing, _____
2. – 4. *See additional lyrics*

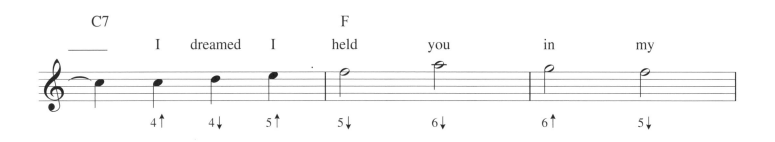

_____ I dreamed I held you in my

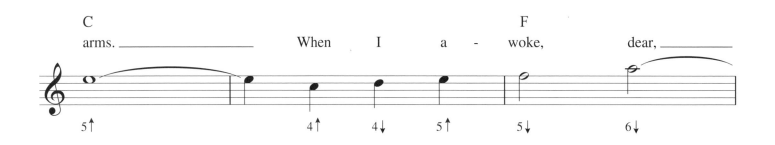

arms. _____ When I a - woke, dear, _____

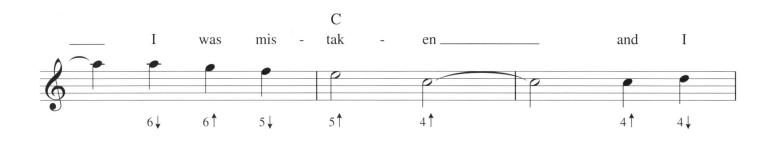

_____ I was mis - tak - en _____ and I

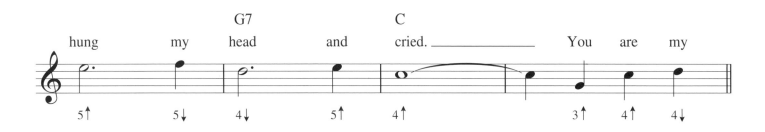

hung my head and cried. _____ You are my

Chorus

Additional Lyrics

2. I'll always love you
   And make you happy
   If you will only say the same.
   But if you leave me
   To love another,
   You'll regret it all some day.

3. You told me once, dear,
   You really loved me
   And no one could come between.
   But now you've left me
   And love another.
   You have shattered all of my dreams.

4. In all my dreams, dear,
   You seem to leave me.
   When I awake my poor heart pains.
   So won't you come back
   And make me happy?
   I'll forgive, dear, I'll take all the blame.

You Are So Beautiful

Words and Music by Billy Preston and Bruce Fisher

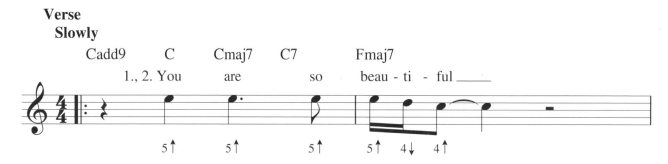

Verse
Slowly

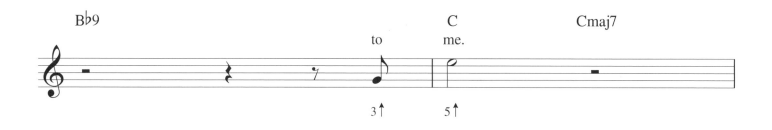

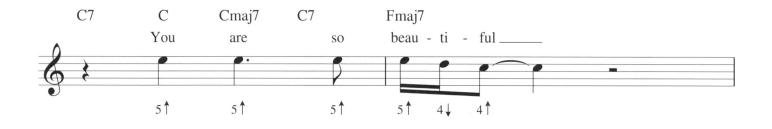

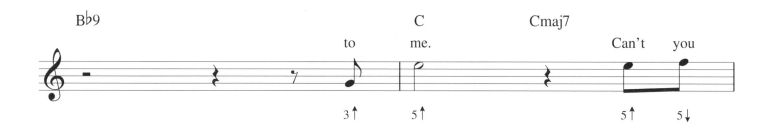

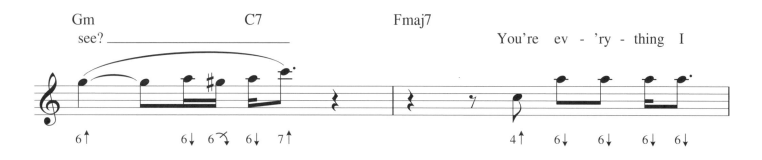

Copyright © 1973 IRVING MUSIC, INC. and ALMO MUSIC CORP.
Copyright Renewed
All Rights Reserved   Used by Permission

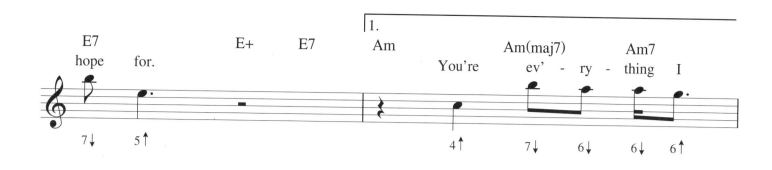

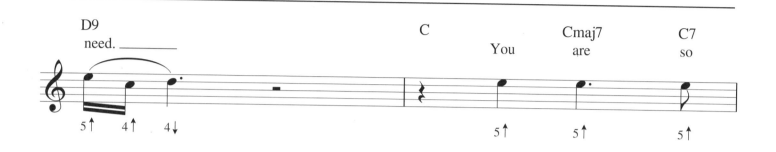

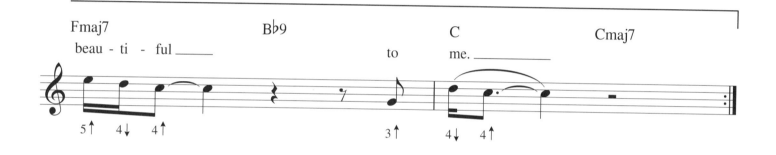

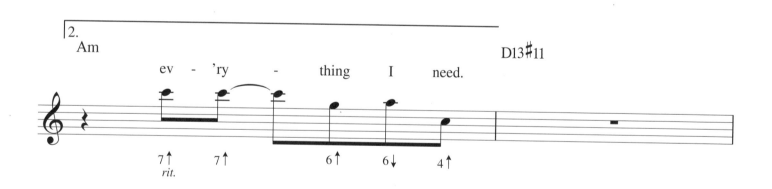

A tempo

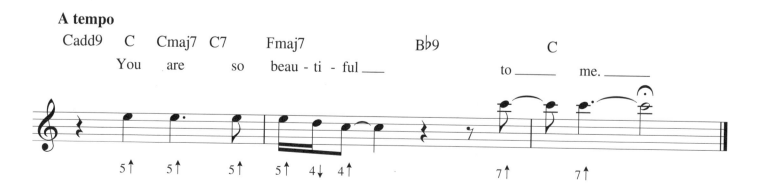

You Are the Sunshine of My Life

Words and Music by Stevie Wonder

Chorus
Moderately

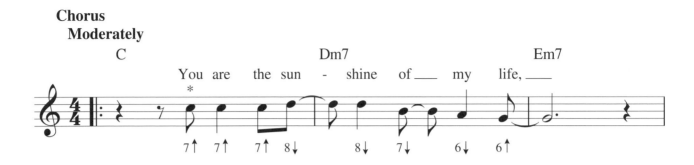

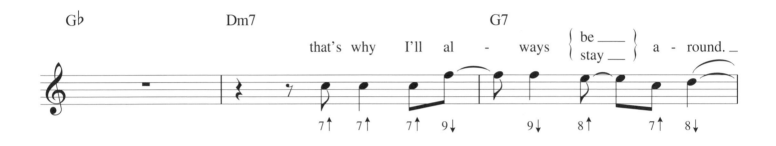

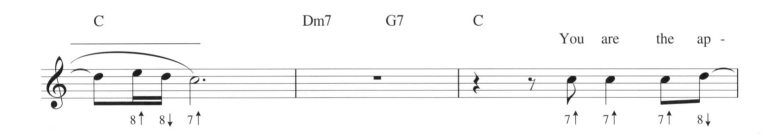

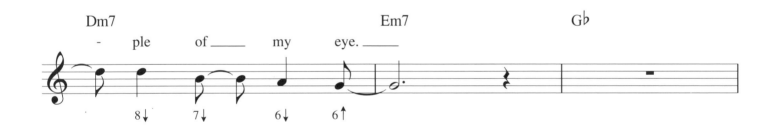

Your Cheatin' Heart

Words and Music by Hank Williams

Verse
Moderately fast

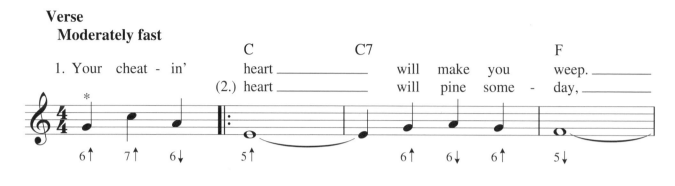

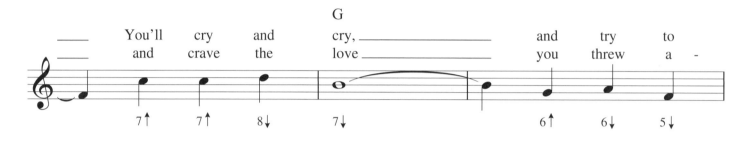

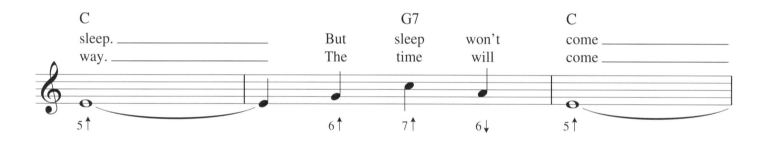

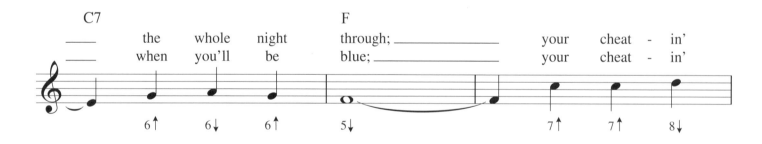

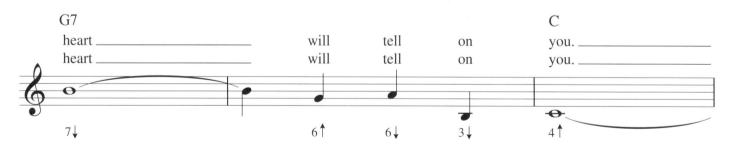

*Song sounds one octave higher than written.

Bridge

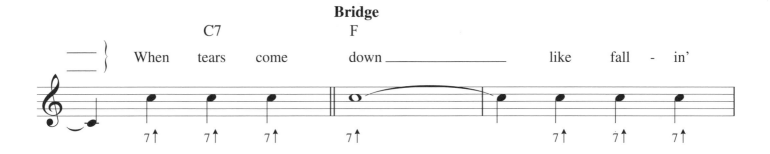

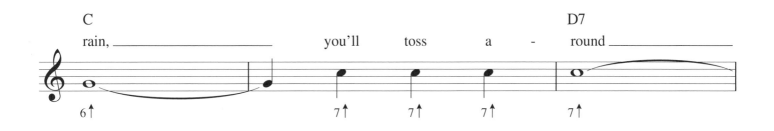

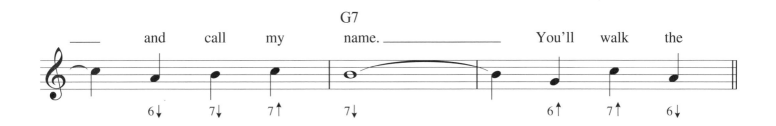

Chorus

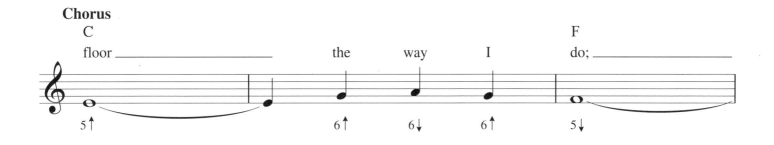

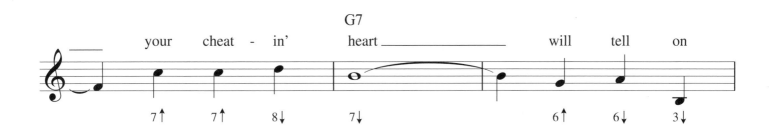

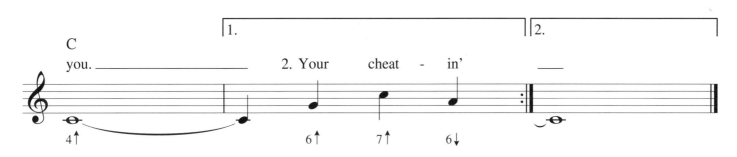

What a Wonderful World

Words and Music by George David Weiss and Bob Thiele

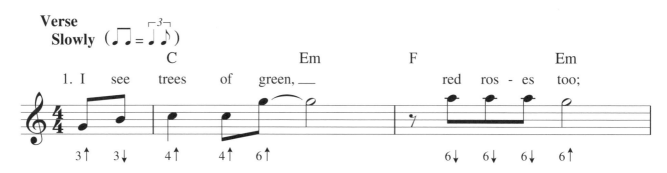

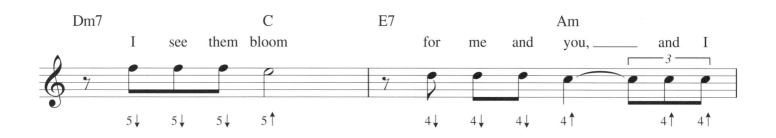

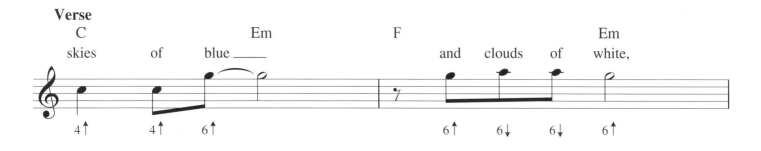

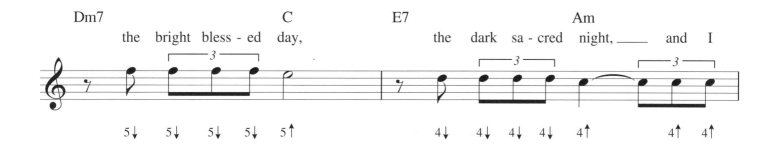

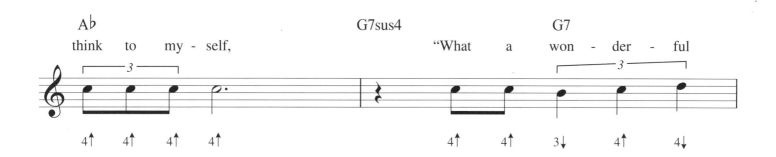

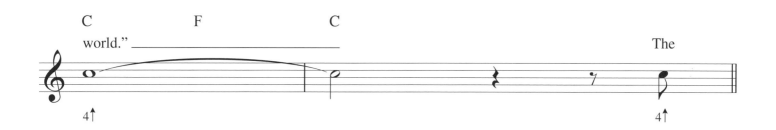

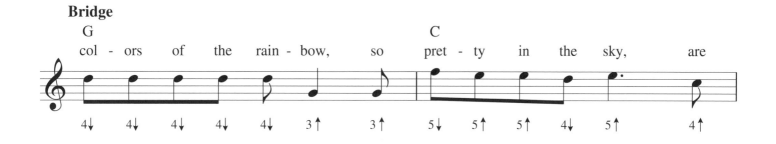

Bridge

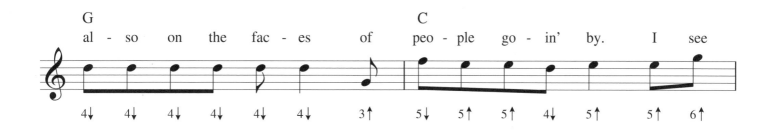

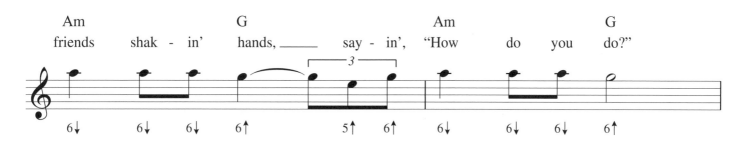

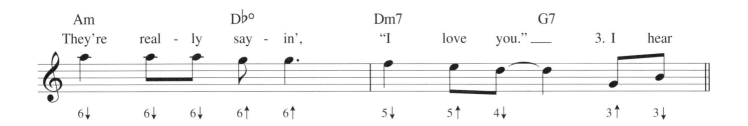

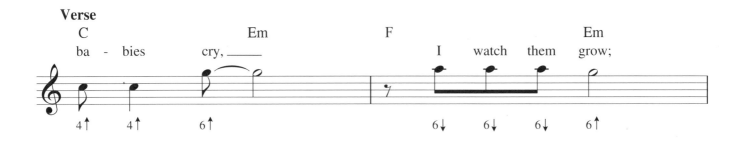

Verse

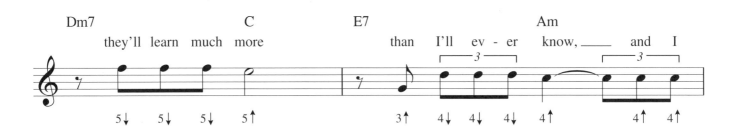

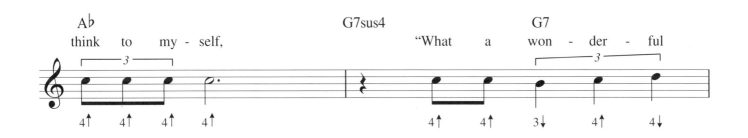

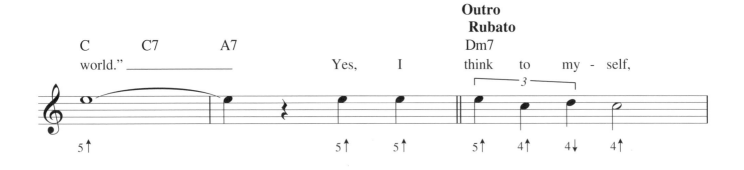

Outro
Rubato

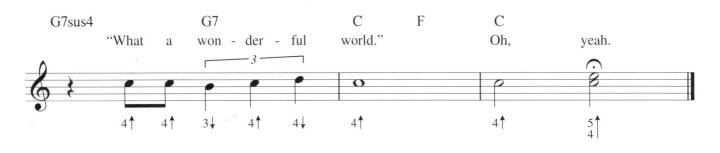